CONTENTS

CONTENTS

YES
WE CAN!

A Community College Guide For
Developing America's Underprepared

Robert H. McCabe

League for Innovation in the Community College
American Association of Community Colleges

The League for Innovation in the Community College is an international organization dedicated to catalyzing the community college movement. The League hosts conferences and institutes, develops Web resources, conducts research, produces publications, provides services, and leads projects and initiatives with more than 750 member colleges, 100 corporate partners, and a host of other government and nonprofit agencies in a continuing effort to make a positive difference for students and communities. Information about the League is available at www.league.org.

The American Association of Community Colleges (AACC) is the primary advocacy organization for the nation's community colleges. The association represents 1,100 two-year, associate degree-granting institutions and more than 10 million students. AACC promotes community colleges through six strategic action areas: national and international recognition and advocacy, learning and accountability, leadership development, economic and workforce development, connectedness across AACC membership, and international and intercultural education. Information about AACC and community colleges may be found at www.aacc.nche.edu.

The opinions expressed in this book are those of the authors and do not necessarily reflect the views of The Pew Charitable Trusts, the League for Innovation in the Community College, or the American Association of Community Colleges.

©2003 League for Innovation in the Community College and American Association of Community Colleges

Requests for permission should be sent to
League for Innovation in the Community College
4505 E. Chandler Boulevard, Suite 250
Phoenix, AZ 85048
e-mail: publications@league.org
fax: (480) 705-8201

Printed in the United States of America.
ISBN 1-931300-34-8

PREFACE
THE COURAGE TO SAY "YES WE CAN!"

In our work with community and technical colleges nationally and internationally, we are regularly taken aback by the commitment and energy educators bring to the challenges faced by our institutions. We can point to powerful examples where teachers and leaders in our field fight through outdated tradition and blinding bureaucracy to build transfer programs and form smooth-functioning articulation agreements for students; embrace change at breakneck speed to adapt curriculum and provide new e-learning delivery systems for the Information Age; respond to national imperatives to create programs that address national workforce shortages in nursing and teacher education; sound the call to arms to support programs in biotechnology, healthcare, and law enforcement to strengthen our national security; and survive and thrive in the face of painful local and state budget cuts that threaten to decrease access to higher education for the least privileged of our society.

Still, there are few examples that move us as much as those instances in which community and technical college educators rage against assumption, innuendo, arrogance, apathy, and misinformation to meet the ever-present and essential need to provide high-quality developmental education. Even in the face of powerful evidence that good policy and practice supporting developmental education is cost effective and socially essential for communities, states, and nations—as well documented in the companion book to this volume, *No One to Waste*—there are still those who claim we cannot make these programs work. In this book, Robert McCabe and a host of colleagues who are leading and teaching in highly successful developmental educational programs shout back: YES WE CAN!

Their courage in developing and implementing these programs is equaled only by the everyday courage of students who take steps through our open doors to access them. Research shows that many of these students are at turning points in their lives. Their stories of succeeding in our developmental education programs often involve overcoming poverty, layoffs, poor primary and secondary schooling, and incredibly complex family and often harrowing life situations. Can we honor their courage? YES WE CAN! And we honor these student efforts here by learning from those educators who are working hard at building programs that work in developmental education.

Mark David Milliron
President and CEO
League for Innovation in the Community College

George Boggs
President and CEO
American Association of Community Colleges

FOREWORD

Yes we can! Most academically deficient students do not lack talent. They lack preparation. Community colleges have the capability to develop these talents for the benefit of the students and our nation. We have no more important mission. Nearly half of entering community college students are underprepared and less than half gain the competencies needed to succeed in standard college courses. We can improve on this limited success. The current high level of interest in developmental education among public decision makers and college leaders is encouraging. This volume is intended to capitalize on that interest. It is a follow-up to the policy study, *The National Study of Community College Remedial Education* (McCabe, 2000).

THE PROJECT

This project of the League for Innovation in the Community College was funded by The Pew Charitable Trusts and directed by Robert H. McCabe.

A national steering committee of professionals experienced with underprepared community college students guided the effort to ensure maximum participation by developmental education practitioners. The project focuses on delivery of services to students.

Over a period of nine months, the Steering Committee developed an outline for this publication. The committee's aim was to explore topics that would be most useful to program directors and practitioners. The education of non-native speakers was excluded because this subject would require a separate project. A chapter is included concerning the relationship of English for Speakers of Other Languages (ESOL) to developmental education.

The guide is a primer on services for underprepared students. It sets forth information on each phase of the program, based on research findings and the practical experiences of professionals who serve underprepared students. In order to have adequate discussion, and because of differing views among the writers, topics such as placement are commented on in more than one chapter.

The book is the work of the steering committee, not of individual writers. Writers with experience in each topic area were commissioned to draft appropriate chapters. In accordance with the committee's core outline, the writers developed detailed outlines. These were circulated to the steering committee and the other writers for comments. Based on the comments, the project director modified and approved the outlines. The writers submitted drafts, and the edited drafts were posted on the project website for a month. Writers, members of the steering committee, and other interested individuals commented on the text, and those comments were considered in the final draft.

The steering committee also identified effective programs and practices. The selected colleges were invited to submit brief program or practice descriptions, and these are included.

The volume is designed to be a practical tool for improving the important services that community colleges provide to underprepared students.

PROJECT STEERING COMMITTEE

Robert H. McCabe, Chair
Senior League Fellow, League for Innovation in the Community College

Charles Brown
Madison Area Technical College (WI)

Mary Darin
Richland College (TX)

Rene Garcia
Miami-Dade Community College (FL)

Teresa Hieronymus
Sinclair Community College (OH)

Chuck Hinz
Kirkwood Community College (IA)

Patricia John
Lane Community College (OR)

Donna McKusick
Community College of Baltimore County (MD)

Gail Miulli
Cascadia Community College (WA)

William Muller
Moraine Valley Community College (IL)

Darlene Nold
Community College of Denver (CO)

Ann Puyana
Valencia Community College (FL)

Nancy Turner
Central Carolina Community College (NC)

THE WRITERS

Susanne Adams
Sandhills Community College (NC)

Jean Conway
Richland College (TX)

Rene Garcia
Miami-Dade Community College (FL)

Sheri Goldstein
Miami Dade Community College (FL)

Janice Hill-Matula
Moraine Valley Community College (IL)

Michael Khirallah
Oakland Community College (MI)

Byron McClenney
Kingsborough Community College (NY)

Donna McKusick
Community College of Baltimore County (MD)

William Muller
Moraine Valley Community College (IL)

Susan Clark Thayer
Suffolk University (NY)

Jacquelyn Tulloch
Academic Systems

Linda Wong
Consultant

ACKNOWLEDGMENTS

I wish to thank Clinton Cooper for assistance in maintaining communications with all the involved parties; Laura Pincus Sekoff for patience with the very difficult task of editing so many writers; and Regina Dodd for being there for whatever was needed. Without the support of the League for Innovation in the Community College, this project would not have been possible. The American Association of Community Colleges was always available for advice and assistance. Finally, I thank my wife Arva for her encouragement and enthusiasm for my work, and for her merciless, insightful, and needed critiques. They really do help.

Robert H. McCabe

1
RISING TO COMMITMENT

No educational program is as misunderstood or underappreciated as community college developmental education. Both legislatures and colleges give it low priority. Yet it is essential to the nation's well being. It is cost-effective, productive, and one of the most important services provided by community colleges. In this rapidly changing world, it is imperative to develop the talents of every American.

Developmental education is essential to achieving that end. It is sound economic and social policy, and it represents the best of our national values.

Community colleges are the most American of institutions. They are agents of democratization, with a core mission to provide opportunity to all. Colleges have committed themselves to every student

> *Developmental education is cost-effective, productive, and one of the most important services provided by community colleges.*

who is admitted. They have a clear obligation to do the best for everyone. Yet in serving underprepared students, more often than not this obligation goes unmet. Institutions underfund programs, hire primarily part-time instructors, and use ineffective educational practices. This is shameful and unacceptable. Community colleges must do better.

Why America Has No One to Waste

As we begin the 21st century, information technology is transforming the world at a breathtaking pace. Our future economy will be built on information-based industries that need a broadly based, highly skilled workforce. Eighty percent of new jobs will require some postsecondary education, yet only 42 percent of today's students leave high school with the necessary skills to begin college-level work (McCabe, 2000). Each year one million students—one in four who enter higher education—are underprepared. More than ever, our future depends on advances in education. Public school performance must dramatically improve so more students graduate from high school with college entry skills.

Even with aggressive school reforms, substantial numbers of young Americans will reach adulthood underprepared for employment in the 21st century. A growing percentage of these individuals will enter college. To succeed, many will need developmental education services. These services pay important benefits. Each year, with an expenditure of only 1 percent of our higher education budgets, institutions successfully remediate more than half a million college students. After remediation, they do as well in standard college courses as those who begin fully prepared. Through developmental education, they hone the skills for quality employment and for becoming positive contributors to our society. Providing effective developmental programs salvages opportunity for underprepared students.

A Changing Nation

America enjoys unprecedented prosperity and technology. Yet to remain competitive in the global economy, we must reverse the growth of what seems to be a permanent underclass and develop a highly skilled workforce. The task of raising the competencies of our citizens falls on the educational system. Community colleges have a particularly important role. They educate the most deficient students—those who would otherwise be lost to our society—and prepare them for employment and personal advancement.

The belief in the value of every human being, the commitment to fully developing the talents of all our citizens, sets us apart from other nations. It is our greatest strength.

In his inaugural address, President George W. Bush described the grandest of our ideals as the promise "that everyone belongs, that everyone deserves a chance, that no insignificant person was ever born… ." That belief in the value of every human being, the commitment to fully develop the talents of all of our citizens, sets us apart from other nations. It is our greatest strength. In the information-rich America of the 21st century, fulfilling that commitment demands universal access to postsecondary education. It redefines the mission of American education and can only be achieved through reinventing the K-12 system and through effective community college developmental education.

Business, Industry, and Work

In the global economy, business and industry operate wherever costs are lowest. Manufacturing is already moving from the United States to countries with lower wages–a trend expected to continue. Sustaining America's future will depend on innovations in the knowledge industries and on developing a more productive workforce. Brainpower and technology can multiply individual productivity to compensate for our higher wages and help America retain economic leadership. The countries that remain competitive in the 21st century will be those with the highest overall literacy and a strong bottom third of its population.

The workplace of tomorrow will be quite different from that of today, a result of both revolutionary and evolutionary changes. Revolutionary changes will take place as new jobs require markedly different and higher competencies. Existing jobs will continue to evolve, requiring different behaviors and job skills from those that employees now possess. Simple jobs will become high performance jobs. Workers will need the capacity to reason through complex processes rather than follow rote instructions or complete the discrete steps of larger processes. These workers will need higher-order information skills as a foundation for lifelong learning.

Our educational system is falling far short of matching that requirement. Throughout the country, businesses report that their workforce is underskilled. They are experiencing shortages of competent job applicants. They have pressured Congress to allow the immigration of 300,000 highly skilled foreign workers each year to fill quality jobs for which Americans are not prepared.

Changing Demographics

By the year 2050, nearly half the population will belong to ethnic minorities, with the most dramatic shift among youths. Thanks to immigration and higher birth rates, Hispanic Americans comprise the fastest growing population. They make up 11 percent of the population today and will represent 25 percent by 2050, increasing from 30 million to 96 million. This growth is remarkable, considering that in 1970, Hispanics accounted for only nine million citizens, or 4 percent of the population.

In terms of our education system, these changes are profound. Poverty has the highest correlation with educational underpreparation, and minorities—especially immigrants—have disproportionately high poverty rates. Tragically, at a time when schools are struggling to raise learning expectations, a greater number of underprepared young people will begin school.

Ethnicity is not the only demographic force at work; the graying of America will be equally important. Today, we are experiencing the impact of the post-World War II baby boom as 76 million Americans prepare to retire. Through 2030, the number of Americans in their prime work years is expected to remain constant at 160 million, while the number of individuals over 65 will increase from 33.5 million to 69.3 million. To support the growing elderly population, all Americans in their prime work years must be highly skilled and increasingly productive.

Lack of Progress for Minorities

Minorities have made some educational progress in recent years, but the achievement gap between minority and majority students is still troubling. Hispanic Americans comprise approximately 14 percent of the 15- to 19-year-old population, but they earn only 7 percent of the associate degrees and 6 percent of the bachelor's degrees. African Americans are approximately 16 percent of the 15- to 19-year-old population, but they earn only 10 percent of the associate degrees and 9 percent of the bachelor's degrees. White non-Hispanics comprise 70 percent of the 15- to 19-year-old population, and they earn 83 percent of the associate degrees and 86 percent of the bachelor's degrees. Hispanic Americans and African Americans lose ground at every step of the educational ladder, from high school graduation and college enrollment to earning degrees and certificates. These results are contrary to America's fundamental goals and represent a great loss of talent that our nation desperately needs.

K-12 School Reform: Not the Whole Answer

The school reform movement that began in the 1980s is finally showing limited progress. The task of preparing all young Americans for universal access to postsecondary education, however, is monumental. Even with expected progress, our secondary schools will not be able to do it all. Today, only 64 percent of young people earn a standard high school diploma; another 18 percent earn an alternate diploma at an average age of 25. A significant gap exists between current high school graduation standards and the competencies needed to begin college. Only 42 percent of young Americans have the competencies necessary to begin college. Unless school performance improves, with the projected demographic changes there will be a decrease to 33 percent. The schools must significantly improve performance if they are to hold their ground or progress.

Community College Developmental Education

Developmental education is one of the most important programs community colleges offer. The evolving educational pattern is a continuum that includes college entry. Four of five Americans will need some postsecondary education, and most will return for upgrading, retraining, or personal growth. The majority will enroll in community colleges. Nearly half of these students have some basic skills deficiency. Community college enrollment will skyrocket and even more students will lack academic preparation. They will depend on community college developmental education as the lifeline to their future.

Who Are the Underprepared Students?

While there are patterns among underprepared students that might suggest a pigeonhole, the remedial population resists an easy solution to designing an effective developmental program. As Boylan, Bonham, and

Bliss (1994) observe, there are more female than male developmental students. Remedial students range in age from 15 to 55. Nearly half are 24 years of age or older. While a high percentage are financially disadvantaged, some are quite wealthy. The majority is composed of white non-Hispanics, but African Americans and Hispanics are overrepresented. Some students are married and some are single.

More than 40 percent of beginning community college students are underprepared, and in some urban colleges this is the situation for three of every four new students (McCabe, 2000). While they are about 9 percent of America's college students, minorities account for 23 percent of the remedial population (Boylan, Bonham, & Bliss, 1994). They are especially overrepresented among the seriously underprepared (McCabe, 2000).

Approximately one-fourth of these students are married, and the average age is approximately 28 (Roueche & Roueche, 1999). Although little solid income data is available, remedial students tend to be at a low socioeconomic level (Roueche & Roueche, 1999). McCabe and Day note, "From kindergarten to college, poverty correlates more closely with academic deficiency than any other factor" (1995, p. 5). Students with physical disabilities represent 10 percent of the population. Immigrants make up a significant percentage of these students and they tend to be academically weak. Many have poor or low high school or GED test scores. The mean cumulative high school grade point average (GPA) of entering community college remedial students is 2.40. Although few take the SAT to enter the community college, one study indicated that 50 percent of remedial students scored 800 or lower on the SAT (Knopp, 1996). In addition, many underprepared students literally have never left their neighborhoods (Roueche & Roueche, 1999) and possess limited knowledge of the world. They also have little family or peer encouragement to advance academically.

Underprepared Students and Results

The nature of academic deficiencies differs dramatically. One-third of the students are deficient in all basic areas, one-third in two of the three basic areas, and one-third in only one area. And there is great variation in the depth of deficiencies. Approximately half of academically deficient students successfully complete remediation. Those who succeed do as well in standard college classes as those who began without deficiencies. One-sixth earn academic associate and bachelor's degrees and one-third earn occupational associate degrees and certificates. Ten years after beginning developmental courses, 98 percent are employed and 90 percent are in jobs above minimal level. Nearly two-thirds are in new technical and office careers, the areas of greatest growth. They commit less than one-third the number of felonies than other Americans with similar demographics. Half are continuing their education.

Cost

Contrary to common belief, developmental education programs are cost effective. They serve one million students a year and successfully remediate half that number for an expenditure of only 1 percent of the national higher education budget and 4 percent of federal student financial aid. The average academically deficient student enrolls in developmental courses for the equivalent of approximately one-fourth of an academic year. In a higher-tuition community college with an annual FTE cost of $6,000 and student fees at 25 percent, the public cost per student for remediation would be $1,125. Considering the productive futures of successfully remediated students, the cost-benefit ratio is exceptional.

Priority

Often, both legislatures and colleges underfund developmental programs. As productive as these programs are, they should and can be successful with more students. To succeed academically, deficient students need more than courses often taught by part-time instructors. They need personal support and integrated programs involving classes, counseling, learning laboratories, and other support services.

It may be natural for academic professionals to be most interested in academically advanced students and to lack interest in the underprepared. For that reason, excellent developmental education programs exist only in colleges where a priority is clearly established by the trustees and the president.

Our nation's future depends upon everyone recognizing the importance of developmental education and raising it to the level of priority it needs and deserves.

2
INSTITUTIONAL AND POLICY ISSUES

*Community college leaders know that remediation is an
inescapable obligation in an institution which has an open-door
admissions policy and which invites enrollment of all high school
graduates and others who can benefit from its programs.*

Ed Gleazer, 1968, p. 58

The assertions made by Ed Gleazer seemed so clear at a time when many new community colleges dotted the American landscape. Approximately 500 institutions had opened in the 1960s, and Gleazer was concerned about the educational opportunities for poor and undereducated citizens. He led the American Association of Junior Colleges (AAJC) to publish *Salvage, Redirection, or Custody? Remedial Education in the Community Junior College* (Roueche, 1968), which was the first major work to focus on remedial programs. The Roueche work prompted others to examine the subject.

Medsker and Tillery (1971, p. 68) observed that community colleges exhibited more concern about and experimentation with developmental education than with any other component of their program. They estimated that 30 to 50 percent of entering students lacked the basic skills required for college-level courses.

By 1992, Cohen (1992, p. 89) suggested that all community colleges were offering some developmental education courses. He referred to courses in English, reading, speech, mathematics, or arithmetic, as well as to special counseling, tutoring, and assistance in study laboratories. These efforts focused on providing access for increasing numbers of underprepared students. Roueche and Roueche (1993) described the circumstances as placing community colleges "between a rock and a hard place" (p.1). Things have not changed; community colleges still face the daunting challenge of how to serve the neediest of students. Whether the students are described as skill-deficient, disadvantaged, nontraditional, at-risk, or underprepared, it is clear that the charge has never been greater. In *No One To Waste*, McCabe (2000) issues the call for a strong commitment to serving the underprepared.

Commitment to the Underprepared

Today, nearly half of entering community college students are academically underprepared. Given this circumstance, Gleazer's argument of more than 30 years ago is now manifest. Yet in spite of its prevalence and importance, one wonders how "the majority of community colleges [do not] have a solid grasp of the extent of the problem, much less have designed and implemented responses that the public and the politics of the day will continue to accept." (Roueche & Roueche, 1999, p. 6).

It is imperative for institutions to assign a high priority to serving the underprepared. The numbers demand commitment and society requires it (McCabe, 2000). How else will students be prepared to enter community college transfer and career programs? Colleges need to see developmental education as a foundation for their mission. The transfer curriculum and increasing numbers of career or occupational programs require higher levels of academic competence at the point of entry. When continuing education, ESL, and GED preparation are added, the four central mission elements can exist in complementary relationships.

Stakeholders

Various stakeholders need to be involved in and educated about the importance of serving the underprepared (Roueche & Roueche, 1999). As the fiscal policymakers for remedial programs, governors and legislatures certainly play a significant role. Mayors and city councils in places such as New York City and Chicago and state and local boards also share a role in policy and funding. Government wants people off welfare and a qualified workforce in place; education can make those goals attainable.

A strong governmental commitment must be paired with an equally strong commitment at all educational levels. Students who struggle in the early grades end up in community college developmental classes. K-12 educators must recognize the cycle of deficiency and partner with the colleges to better prepare students. Ultimately, such a coherent linkage could significantly reduce the need for developmental programs.

Poverty has a noted connection to poor student performance. Because of that reality, a strong case can be made for partnerships with community-based organizations that reach the impoverished in cities and towns. They can be called on to help the struggling student. Chambers of commerce and business groups interested in hiring skilled employees could also contribute to developmental education. These somewhat nontraditional stakeholders could join the more traditional players in creating a powerful coalition concerned about successful developmental education at the community college.

It is time to get beyond the blame-the-victim approach and the arguments about paying twice (K-12 and higher education) to educate the same person. Whether we like it or not, remediation is an essential component of higher education. It is also cost effective. More than 30 years of research suggest that the community college is the appropriate place for this form of education. If the effort fails, society faces increased costs for social dependency, prisons, and a less competitive workforce. It is time for the colleges to decide to do it, and do it well.

Master plans, strategic plans, and operational plans all need to stress the importance of successful outcomes in developmental programs. Ambitious institutions should consider the goal of leveling the playing field for those who start in remedial courses. It is possible for them to graduate and transfer at the same rates as better-prepared students. The Institute for Higher Education Policy (1998, p. 11) notes, "Data seem to indicate that remediation is, in fact, quite effective at improving the chances of collegiate success for underprepared students."

Organizing for the Task

A recent survey by the American Association of Community Colleges (Shults, 2000) provided an overview of remedial programs. More than 90 percent of community colleges offer remedial courses in mathematics, reading, and writing, while less than one-third offer remedial science. Sixty-one percent of the responding institutions house remedial courses by subject area. Twenty-five percent of the respondents report offering remedial courses in a separate department, and 13 percent report offerings through one academic department such as English or mathematics. The survey did not deal with special learning laboratories or special student support services. While the study's sample may not be nationally representative, the publication does provide a starting point for organizing a developmental education effort. Roueche and Roueche (1999) describe a successful foundation:

> Most of what we know is that a total program approach to the complex needs of at-risk students–systematic approach–has the greatest potential for success. Moreover, the program should be but one part of an institutionwide commitment to success for all students that includes student development professionals collaborating with faculty and staff to implement policies that will improve student retention, achievement, and graduation rates. (p. 29)

Taking this total-program approach is obviously more difficult in the 74 percent of AACC respondent colleges where courses are offered in separate departments or one host department. Yet good organization alone does not make a successful program. Even if an institution establishes a separate remedial department, it must also include learning skills and student support services.

The recent study by McCabe (2000, p. 46) found that only six of 25 institutions studied revised their remedial programs in the past 10 years. He asserts that effective work in this area is "not a mysterious proposition. We know how to do it. We simply do not use what we know." Roueche and Roueche (1999, p. 29) also discuss major findings from studies over a long period of time. From these two summaries, 16 steps have been identified that would be incorporated in an effective program (See Figure 2.1, p. 25.)

FIGURE 2.1

16 STEPS FOR AN EFFECTIVE DEVELOPMENTAL PROGRAM

1. Avoid the negative connotation of *remedial*, choosing a more positive term like developmental or preparatory to describe a program for underprepared students.

2. Adopt a centralized approach, or at least carefully coordinate the various units involved in program delivery.

3. Adopt goals for the total program effort, even if there is not a single remedial unit.

4. Provide professional development for all faculty and staff who work with underprepared students.

5. Recognize that at-risk students need structure in courses and support services.

6. Recognize the importance of student orientation for new enrollees.

7. Incorporate counseling, study skills, and learning communities or cohort groups in the program.

8. Integrate the work of tutors and mentors with carefully selected faculty members.

9. Address the issues of assessment, placement, late registration, and simultaneous enrollment in college-level courses, including mandatory assessment and mandatory placement.

10. Establish consistency between exit standards for remedial courses and entry standards for college-level courses.

11. Provide supplemental learning opportunities, particularly for skill practice.

12. Find the appropriate use of technology and media to support student learning.

13. Consider a case management approach for the least prepared students.

14. Embrace a variety of approaches and methods in program delivery.

15. Commit to program evaluation and the dissemination of results.

16. Expand and enhance pre-enrollment activity with the public schools.

Institutional Policy Issues

If an institution is serious about properly serving its underprepared population, it must assess all entering students. The concern is whether a student is prepared to profit from instruction in a particular course or program. The literature clearly advocates such testing, but many community colleges struggle over the requirement for part-time, evening, or off-campus enrollees (these issues are discussed in Chapter 3, "Assessment and Placement"). Though the logistics may be challenging, these students need evaluation as much as any other students. Once an institution makes the commitment to entry assessment, it faces the issue of whether or not to mandate placement. Again, the literature makes a clear case for mandatory placement. Institutions serious about following course prerequisites must be equally serious about honoring assessment results. It does not benefit students to permit them to enroll in courses for which they are underprepared. This can only result in high rates of failure and dropout or the compromising of college standards to accommodate the underpreparedness of students.

It does not benefit students to permit them to enroll in courses for which they are underprepared.

Unfortunately, concerns about enrollment numbers and late registration frequently drive the discussion about mandatory assessment and placement. The most underprepared students are likely to be the people in our society whose lives are not orderly. They are not as apt to plan ahead, particularly when it comes to the lead time required to apply for financial aid. We do not, however, serve them well if they are thrust into learning activities without proper orientation and a structured environment. Late-starting courses and open-entry, open-exit options can serve those who arrive too late to have a chance to be successful in traditionally scheduled classes.

Simultaneous enrollment in college-level courses for those needing some remediation must also be considered if student success rates are to be improved. At the heart of this issue is whether students' reading and writing ability and numeracy skills match course requirements, including text materials. The question is, can students handle the academic work?

Similarly, the intensity and frequency of writing assignments or the numeracy skills required should be taken into account when considering simultaneous enrollment for those involved in developmental courses. At the very least, colleges must closely monitor and advise students who are simultaneously enrolled. The creation of learning communities for a cohort of developmental students can provide an appropriate way for a college-level course to be paired with developmental courses.

While the logistics of assessment, placement, and curriculum issues are important, quality faculty and counselors are essential to a developmental education program's success. An assignment to work in these programs should be prestigious. No one who is not committed and passionate about the task should be working with underprepared students. This is not the place for new faculty members straight out of graduate school, unless they are specifically prepared for this work. Part-time faculty members need ongoing professional development opportunities in order to make their best contributions.

By facing the institutional issues described, colleges can create a base from which to develop strategies for success with underprepared students.

Strategies for Success

Once a community college addresses institutional concerns and adopts a total program approach, it must devise standards or competencies for remedial courses, as well as entry standards for college courses. Examples might be as follows:

- Students write and speak using conventional grammar, usage, sentence structure, punctuation, capitalization, and spelling.

- Students use algebraic methods to explore, model, and describe patterns and functions involving numbers, shapes, data, and graphs in problem-solving situations, and to communicate the reasoning used in solving problems.

These examples could be among the standards for graduation from high school as well. Once a community college clearly defines the desired outcomes, it becomes possible to structure learning activities to achieve them. The best efforts, backed by the literature, match the way students learn with alternative approaches to instructional delivery.

A high-tech, high-touch approach that genuinely relates to the needs of underprepared students is one promising way to assist in student learning. The Community College of Denver, for example, has built a benchmark program. After 10 years of work to improve student success, the college used information technology with impressive results. In 1999, its Academic Support Center had 180 active tutors (peer and professional) and 180 computers in support of developmental students. If institutions engage in multiyear efforts to improve results in remediation, then they will have nothing to fear when government, business, and citizens call for accountability.

Accountability

Cohort tracking of entering students is fundamental to creating effective programs. The following questions apply:

- What percentage of an entering cohort needs to take one or more developmental courses?
- How many of those taking developmental courses are successful (GPA of 2.0) in the first term?
- How many are retained for the next term?
- How do the previous two rates compare to those in the original cohort who did not require remediation?
- What is the fall-to-fall retention rate for the developmental portion of the cohort?
- What percentage of the developmental portion of the cohort completes the developmental sequence?
- How do those who complete the developmental sequence perform in subsequent courses such as English composition and college algebra?
- How do those from the original cohort who did not need remediation perform in the same courses?
- How do graduation rates (three-year to six-year) for the developmental portion of the cohort compare to the rates for those in the cohort who did not need remediation?
- What is the average number of terms (or years) required for students to complete the developmental sequence?
- Are there differences in outcomes within the cohort on the basis of race, ethnicity, gender, or age?

Parity for all students should be the goal of community colleges. In any given year, these questions can pinpoint areas requiring special attention. The result will create a culture of evidence that will guide the institution.

Implications

People in a position to influence policy need to understand the stakes. Legislators, members of state coordinating or policy boards, members of city or county legislative bodies with a community college role, and members of local boards of trustees all need to be educated about the issues.

Even if government officials fail to face up to the issues, college presidents must push for the appropriate priority. They can be certain that resources are allocated for the work, and must insist on the evaluation of results. Faculty leaders should see the results and be given the opportunity to talk about how to improve student success rates. In an era when high skills will be required for high wages, societal requirements demand that community colleges transform their efforts with underprepared students.

If community colleges do not rise to the occasion, who will?

3
ASSESSMENT AND PLACEMENT

The need to remediate is a drive to help students succeed, not only academically but also in the work world, where employers frequently decry their employees' lack of basic skills. But how should institutions identify those who need developmental education?

Candidates for developmental education share certain characteristics. Although the majority of these students are White non-Hispanics, minorities are overrepresented. A significant number are foreign-born or first-generation college students who work,many of them full-time; have a poor academic record; and suffer a low self-image (Shults, 2000; McCabe, 2000). Formal assessment is typically used to determine the need for developmental course placement. Implementation of a placement program, however, requires a variety of decisions including what to assess, how to assess it, and whom to assess.

An institution's attitude regarding developmental education and underprepared students makes a critical difference in the success of its programs. Students frequently resist remedial placements because they consider them an additional burden—unnecessary courses that will slow down achievement of their goals. This concern can be overcome through the positive attitude of the faculty and staff. Students must believe that they will benefit from the developmental program. Facts make a difference. Students can be shown that the competencies they learn in developmental courses will result in gains in academic success.

What to Assess

In theory, curriculum should drive assessment. Course content should dictate what skills are required and in turn what to assess. As a result of legislative or other external directives, this sequence is sometimes reversed.

Whether an institution selects an existing instrument or develops a new one, educators often modify the curriculum to reflect what will be assessed.

The areas that colleges are most likely to assess for placement in developmental education are writing, reading comprehension, and mathematical ability. They are skills required across every curriculum and program at the postsecondary level.

The primary purpose of assessment and subsequent remediation is to improve academic performance. Other areas, however, including learning styles, study skills, and affective variables such as attitudes and self-image also impact academic performance.

Instructional delivery rarely aligns with the learning styles of students. Practical considerations, such as dealing with groups of students with diverse learning styles, frequently preclude this from happening. Nevertheless, assessment in this area may be useful if only to allow students to discover for themselves how they learn best. Students can apply this knowledge as they prepare for classes, study for tests, or seek assistance. In addition, colleges are developing greater capacity to provide learning arrangements geared to different learning styles. Instruments such as the *Learning and Study Strategies Inventory* (Weinstein, Schulte, & Palmer, 1987) and the *Survey of Study Habits and Attitudes* (Brown & Holtzman, 1967) can be used for these purposes.

Counseling is a critical element in assisting developmental students. Unfortunately, institutions rarely provide for adequate counseling. Instruments such as the *College Student Inventory* (Stratil, 1988) and the *Inventory for Counseling and Development* (Giddan, Creech, & Lovell, 1988) can assist with this process. They can help pinpoint nonacademic areas of need and provide specific approaches to remediate these nonacademic areas. As noted, entry-level course placement programs seldom use these tests, even though evidence suggests that such remediation is indeed possible (e.g., Haught, Hill, Walls, & Nardi, 1998).

How to Assess

Most frequently, assessment programs use standardized tests. These instruments have been normed under specific conditions and with specific groups. This assumes that test performance can be generalized to comparable groups if administered and scored under the same (or standardized) conditions.

The most popular format for entry-level course placement is the multiple-choice test administered via a paper-and-pencil format. These tests are linear in nature, meaning that all test takers view the same items in the same order. In the last decade, computer-based tests have become increasingly popular.

Some computer tests simply transfer test items to the computer screen, thereby remaining linear. Adaptive tests take a different approach. The test software gauges an individual's performance on one question to determine the next question. Items on these tests are calibrated for difficulty. An algorithm establishes a procedure whereby an item answered correctly is followed by a more difficult question, and a less difficult question follows an item answered incorrectly. The process continues until the program gathers enough information to judge the test taker's skill level.

These adaptive assessments provide significant benefits. They take less time and, since there is no consistent pattern of questions, students can take them at any time. Assessment sessions do not need to be scheduled. (An excellent description of adaptive tests can be found in Wainer, 1990.)

Colleges need to consider several factors in selecting an instrument, including the psychometric properties of the test (i.e., reliability and validity), the logistics of test administration (i.e., how the test is administered and scored), and cost of the test itself as well as personnel and equipment.

Reliability and Validity

The instruments selected must be appropriate for the task. Deciding whether this is the case begins by examining reliability and validity. Reliability refers to consistency throughout the test, from one form of the test to another, or both. Educators express reliability as a correlation ranging from 0.00 (no consistency) to 1.00 (perfect consistency) and measure it in several ways (Vogt, 1993). One approach is to establish consistency by testing the same group of students on alternate forms of the test (i.e., test-retest reliability). Another approach is to offer a single administration of the test to establish consistency and use statistical procedures to determine reliability (i.e., split-half reliability). The reliability of a test should be at least .80, with a reliability of .90 or above required when important decisions are made on the basis of test scores (Nunnally, 1978).

Validity is the extent to which a test measures what it purports to measure. It can take several forms, two of which are most relevant for developmental course placement. Predictive or criterion-related validity is the extent to which a test adequately predicts academic performance. It is expressed as a correlation between scores and some measure of performance—most commonly, course grade. Content validity is the degree to which test items represent the skills in the specified subject area (Rudner, 1994). It is not a statistical property but the collective judgment of a panel of experts who determine that a test represents the skills domain it purports to measure (Vogt, 1993).

Logistics of Test Administration

The best test is reliable and valid and is also easy to administer. Testing time should be long enough to assess the subject and yield useful information, but not so long as to make it impractical or fatigue test takers. Obtaining results should also be relatively easy. Machine-scanned answer sheets can generate results in a relatively short time. Computer-based tests usually produce results instantly.

Costs

Even the most psychometrically accurate test will not be used if the costs of the materials themselves (e.g., booklets, answer sheets), personnel to administer the test and score the test and provide storage and retrieval of scores, and equipment necessary to administer or score the test prove prohibitive.

Other Issues

In addition to showing adequate reliability and validity, a test should be free from systematic bias based on factors such as gender or ethnicity.

Another important consideration involves the accommodations the test provides for students with special needs. Disabled students must have the same opportunity as other students to demonstrate their skills. Test forms should be available in Braille, large-print and audio format. When appropriate, colleges should provide a writer to record answers for those with limited mobility and sign language interpreters for the hearing impaired.

Paper-and-Pencil Versus Computer-Adaptive Tests

The mainstay of standardized testing–the paper-and-pencil test–is being challenged by the increasing popularity of computer-adaptive tests. Although both offer advantages and disadvantages, the trend seems to drift toward the latter.

Computer-adaptive tests offer several advantages. These include greater flexibility in administration, quicker and more efficient assessment, and almost instant availability of results. Most important, since the questions vary for each student, the tests can be taken at any time. Test sessions do not have to be scheduled. The cost of purchasing and maintaining the equipment is a disadvantage. Further, the additional administrative flexibility and limited work stations may extend the hours of testing and require additional personnel. Two of the most popular computer-adaptive tests are the Computerized Placement Test–part of the Accuplacer system developed by the College Board (1995)–and COMPASS, developed by ACT (2001). (See Figure 3.1 p. 36.)

Writing Samples

Faculty often advocate inclusion of a writing sample. However, such a sample is expensive. Evaluation is time consuming and may delay activities such as orientation, advisement, and registration. Further, institutions may have trouble finding qualified readers during certain periods throughout the year. Samples may not be scored consistently and reliably. The high cost is the greatest issue.

In the last few years, educators have turned to computer programs that purport to score writing samples more efficiently and consistently. A prominent example is Write Placer Plus, developed by the College Board as part of its Accuplacer system (College Board, 2001). While it offers almost immediate results and unlimited availability, the program still needs to inspire confidence in users–especially faculty.

FIGURE 3.1   PAPER-AND-PENCIL VERSUS COMPUTER-ADAPTIVE TESTS

COMPUTER-ADAPTIVE TESTS

ADVANTAGES

- Greater flexibility regarding administration; students do not need to begin and end together
- Immediate results
- Electronic transfer of scores
- Dissipation of traffic to other areas such as advisement or orientation
- Fewer opportunities for cheating
- Untimed nature better for nontraditional and older students
- Reduction of items and time to place students
- Larger and more frequently refreshed items
- Easier to retest, as items will be different
- Incorporation of additional local questions and tests (e.g., essay, demographics)
- Testing sessions not required
- Generally presentable to students one test item at a time, reducing test anxiety
- Flexibility an advantage in testing students with special needs

DISADVANTAGES

- Requires capital investment to acquire and replace equipment
- May require additional staff as more as flexibility calls for more hours of availability
- Requires investment in network software and hardware
- Requires technical and computer support
- May require accommodations for students with special needs
- Testing capacity limited by the number of work stations

PENCIL-AND-PAPER TESTS

ADVANTAGES

- Usually less expensive
- Can assess large groups at one time
- Can control scheduling and personnel
- Format generally more familiar to faculty, staff, and students
- May require fewer personnel

DISADVANTAGES

- Timing is rigid
- Everyone must start and end together
- Students view the same items in the same order
- Item pool is relatively smaller
- Requires more supervision to ensure test takers do their own work
- Is less secure since test booklets can be lost

Whom to Assess

Colleges may want to make assessment and subsequent course placement mandatory for all students. This may not be possible, for practical and perhaps even political considerations. In the case of mandatory testing and placement, a system must be secure to prevent circumvention of established policies. To that end, registration holds should be in place to prevent students from registering until they are assessed or have taken the required courses, or both.

Mandatory testing and placement is essential to the students' best interest and to maintaining a quality academic program. Regardless of administrative difficulties, the college must limit the exceptions. There are, however, categories of students who probably should be exempt. These include students with adequate SAT or ACT scores and those with associate or higher degrees. Figure 3.2 presents categories suggesting whom to assess and whom to exempt.

FIGURE 3.2 WHOM TO ASSESS AND WHOM TO EXEMPT

MANDATORY ASSESSMENT REQUIRED

- All degree-seeking students
- All students enrolling in any English or mathematics class
- All students registering beyond a limited number of cumulative credits–perhaps six
- All students with test scores that are more than two years old
- All high school students seeking concurrent enrollment

RECOMMENDED EXEMPTIONS

- Students who have earned an associate degree or higher
- Qualified transient students
- Students who have previously successfully completed required courses
- Students with suitable scores on the SAT, ACT, or other recognized instruments

Establishing Placement Scores

Once an institution selects a testing instrument, it still must establish placement scores. This is as important as the selection of an appropriate test. Criticism directed at a test is frequently misplaced since the problem may lie with the placement scores and not the test itself.

In some states, legislative mandates determine placement scores, thereby precluding institutions from setting their own. Politicians perceive such action as guaranteeing consistency across institutions. These placement scores, however, generally only distinguish between college-level and remedial courses. Institutions may still need to establish additional placement scores for the various levels of developmental courses. In addition to the academic and psychometric issues of establishing placement scores, colleges confront practical considerations. Mandatory assessment and course placement could result in significant enrollment shifts within an institution. The number of students requiring remedial placement based on proposed placement scores, for example, could strain the available resources such as space and personnel. While these considerations should not drive placement decisions, institutions need to account for them in their planning.

Empirical derivation of placement scores can be achieved through a variety of approaches. Livingston and Zieky (1982) provide an excellent summary of these methods, including step-by-step descriptions. No matter how placement scores are established, they require continuous database review and evaluation.

Course Placement Beyond Basic Skills

Some specific course areas may use placement scores. These include courses in which the content places high demands on reading, writing, or mathematical ability, such as natural science courses (chemistry, biology, physics), selected business courses (finance and accounting), and allied health courses.

Since developmental students have needs beyond refining their basic skills, most would benefit from student life courses. These courses address study, test-taking, and time-management skills; they also provide students with an orientation to the college's policies and procedures. At their best, they foster a connection between students and instructors. In many instances, these courses become vehicles for providing group counseling and improving retention and overall academic performance (Morris, 1998 & 2001).

Student deficiencies vary widely. Therefore colleges must determine what courses are appropriate for students who are not deficient in all areas. If the student is deficient only in mathematics, the situation is relatively easy to address. Students can enroll in an assortment of college-level courses in which the math is not essential.

The situation is much more challenging when students are deficient in reading, writing, or both. In theory, all college-level courses require competency in these areas. In many courses—including some in data processing, music, art, physical education, and foreign languages—competency may be less of an issue.

Placement and Diagnosis

Placement usually means enrolling students in courses consistent with their skills and geared to ensuring at least a reasonable chance of success in subsequent classes. Diagnosis refers to specific identification of students' particular strengths and weaknesses. While better instruments are being developed, today no tests provide quality diagnostics. In the absence of formal instruments, the faculty has to evaluate student needs based on class assessments. The goal should be not only to identify specific levels but also to match the levels to appropriate instructional strategies and materials.

Why Evaluate Developmental Education Programs?

As higher education moves toward greater accountability, many states are tying performance-based funding to student outcomes rather than to enrollment. Often, these legislative changes came about because colleges were unwilling to evaluate themselves. Institutions now have no choice but to respond to the external examinations.

But there is a more important reason to evaluate than responding to legislative demands. Developmental education programs must continuously evaluate results as a basis for improvement. The task of developmental education is especially difficult, and unrelenting attention to improvement is essential.

Effectiveness of Placement Scores

Data must be collected to determine the effectiveness of placement scores. Are students being placed correctly within the curriculum? Are students who complete developmental education better prepared to perform at a college level?

Perhaps the ideal way to directly establish placement scores is to allow everyone to experience the criterion regardless of performance on the predictor (Nunnally, 1978). If the criterion is performance in a college-level freshman English class, all students register for this class regardless of score. After faculty issue grades, a correlation is established between scores and grades. If the correlation is high, the relationship between test scores and course grades corresponds and the test is a good predictor of performance.

As this misplaces some students and puts them at risk of failure, the approach is rarely used in an educational setting. Alternatives exist. One is to calculate the proportion of students successfully completing the course by individual score. Another establishes baselines before implementing new scores; administrators can compare students' rates of improvement and completion before and after mandatory placement or change in placement scores. This allows an assessment of progress across time. A third approach compares the success or completion rates of those who take the placement tests with those of students who enter the course through prerequisites or other means. To determine any differential impact, data should also be analyzed for significant subgroups such as gender, ethnicity, and age.

Course Grades

Course grades are the most common measure of student learning. Researchers, however, have criticized their reliability. Instructors in different courses at an array of institutions may grade differently. Demonstrated grade inflation has also brought course grades into question. Nevertheless, almost all institutions operationally define success in terms of grades. Other evaluative techniques may be just as relevant in measuring student outcomes. These include semester and cumulative grade point average and completion of significant milestones within a program.

Performance of Remediated Students

The effectiveness of a remedial program rests on the performance of students in subsequent coursework. Their performances can be compared against those of students who needed remediation but did not complete it, or against the performances of students who did not require remediation. Other measurable outcomes are achievements of significant academic milestones such as completing college-level English and math courses, completing the general education core, passing a state-mandated exit test, earning a degree, and successfully performing after transferring to a four-year college. Additional outcomes relating to remediation efforts include type of employment and earnings.

Completion and Success Rates

Completion rates and success rates are related but different concepts. *Completion rate* refers to the proportion of students receiving a grade (i.e., not withdrawing from the course). *Success rate* is the proportion of students who earned a grade that would allow them to progress to the next course or level. Thus, a student earning an F would count as a completion but not a success. Both rates are important. In institutions with a liberal withdrawal policy, the number of students withdrawing may mask the nature of the problem unless the completion rate is also analyzed.

Using Cohorts

Practical considerations frequently preclude an account of all students in an evaluation. One solution is to follow a cohort–a group of individuals who have something in common–through the curriculum to assess progress at relevant points. In this case, what they have in common is placement in developmental courses. Institutions may further group the cohort by specific categories such as the amount of remediation needed or by demographic variables such as ethnicity. (See Figure 3.3 on p. 42.)

FIGURE 3.3

OPERATIONAL DEFINITIONS FOR SELECTED STUDENT OUTCOMES

End-of-Course Grade: Grade assigned at the conclusion of a course. The grade earned indicates whether the student has met requirements and can progress to the next course, or whether the student must repeat the course.

Course Completion Rate: Proportion of students not withdrawing from a course. A student earning a failing grade would contribute toward the completion rate.

Course Success Rate: Proportion of students earning a grade that either fulfills course requirements (and precludes repeating it) and/or allows progress to the next level.

Program Completion Rate: Proportion of a cohort group that completes requirements for a particular program.

Retention Rate: Proportion of students from a cohort group who re-enroll in a subsequent semester. It could use different language for terms, such as fall to winter or fall to fall.

Exit Tests

As an alternative to course grades, colleges can use other methods to certify that students have reached the required skill level. While there is debate concerning retesting students on an alternative form of the placement instrument, many find it to be a practical approach. Computer-adaptive tests are particularly useful for this purpose. Another approach is to require students to pass an exit test. Sometimes it may be a departmental examination developed by faculty. In some cases, an exit test is a legislative mandate.

Using Surveys for Evaluation

Institutions should also conduct assessments on other aspects of developmental education, including student evaluation of instruction as well as tutoring, academic advisement, labs, and other support services. They can be completed easily through surveys and questionnaires done in class or at the point of service.

Programs can also use surveys and questionnaires to assess faculty members' perceptions regarding the accuracy of the placement of students in their classes. Faculty in nonremedial areas should also be surveyed about their experience with postdevelopmental students. The evaluations can explore whether exiting students are prepared for their courses or whether individual students in English, mathematics, and reading are placed too high or too low. Their responses can be measured against grades earned by students and a pattern can emerge.

Another way to evaluate services and gather valuable information is through focus groups. These provide a way for more in-depth data gathering than surveys or questionnaires. Focus groups can be used with faculty, staff, and students. Stewart and Shamdasani (1990) provide an excellent source of information on focus groups.

4
THE DEVELOPING HUMAN BEING: NONACADEMIC CONSIDERATIONS

Well-organized developmental programs that assess, place, and instruct students using a variety of teaching and learning options form a solid base for remediation in the community college. If institutions are truly committed to being successful with high-risk students, however, they must think holistically. At-risk students come to college with diverse needs that stand-alone services or classes will not meet (Roueche & Roueche, 1999). A solid developmental program is not only about academics; it concerns students' personal growth and development. When programs ignore personal issues, they limit students' prospects for academic advancement. The college must consider a broader institutional commitment to the development of human beings.

The Underprepared Population

Nearly half the students entering community colleges enroll in one or more developmental classes. The dropout rate in these courses is high—as much as 25 percent per semester—and only one of two students completes remediation. As Grubb explains, "While it's plausible that dreary teaching is the reason, the difficult lives of many community college students—including financial problems, child care problems, transportation problems, other family problems. . .and the pervasive indecision of experimenting and uncommitted students—surely play important roles" (1998, p. 22).

> *A solid developmental program is not only about academics; it concerns student's personal growth and development.*

D. Patrick Saxon and Hunter R. Boylan (1998) provide insights into this very diverse population. Research on the noncognitive characteristics of developmental students is limited; in fact, aside from academic competencies and family income, these students appear to be very much like most other community college students. There is evidence, however, that although equally motivated, remedial students have more difficulty identifying with an academic environment and regulating learning strategies. They are typically uncertain about their goals and have little academic direction (Thompson, 1998). In addition, remedial students tend to lack higher-order thinking skills needed to survive in an academic setting, and they need careful assessment, intensive counseling, and other structured learning assistance services (Reed, Makarem, Wadsworth, & Shaughnessy, 1994; Shaughnessy & Moore, 1994). Interestingly, remedial students tend to possess many of the same noncognitive characteristics associated with most first-generation community college students and minority students who attend predominantly White colleges.

The American Commitment

While this diversity makes the developmental population difficult to serve, it also makes serving them imperative. Lavin and Hyllegard (1996) indicate that remediation and development of productive citizens represent a promise that historically has been an American way of life. Without the promise of remediation, "the longstanding contract between the United States and its least powerful citizens is violated"(p. 25).

Remedial students have more difficulty identifying with an academic environment and regulating learning strategies.

Higher education has traditionally been exclusive rather than inclusive. In the past 20 years, however, the number of high school graduates attending college has risen from 49 percent to 63 percent (McGrath, 2001). In addition, institutions recognize that their populations include more minorities, more first-generation students, more students who must take jobs to cover school costs, and more students who lack basic skills (McGrath, 2001). Although we know that 80 percent of the 21st century workforce will need some postsecondary education (McCabe & Day, 1998), 60 percent of these students will never complete their degrees, and only half will remain after the first year (McGrath, 2001).

What can institutions do to keep these students? Research indicates that only one-third of them leave school for academic reasons (Tinto, 1993) and that the institution's environment strongly influences their decisions (Astin, 1993). What happens outside the classroom has a strong impact on student success and whether a student decides to tough it out. If institutions want the opportunity to develop human beings, they must become more humane themselves.

An Institutional Commitment

Strong administrative support generally equals a strong developmental program. Roueche and Roueche (1999) argue that an institutionwide commitment to remedial education is a critical factor in a program's success. A college asserts its commitment by accepting remediation as a major element in its mission and goals, allocating appropriate resources and publicly supporting the developmental program. Administrative commitment is often overlooked as a nonacademic consideration to the success of a remedial program. Specifically, in what ways can an institution intervene in its services to high-risk students and promote the development of human beings?

A college's attitude toward and support of underprepared individuals can be quite visible on campus. Where are the remedial facilities located? What academic support services are contiguously housed? How do the facilities look? How do they feel? Developmental classes located in the basement area of a remote building alienate students from the mainstream population and deliver the message that those students are not important. According to Vincent Tinto (Spann, 1990, p. 20), "Institutions are communities, not systems," and programs for at-risk students should "be centralized and provide integrative, not segregated, experiences for their students. When students are set apart, they are stigmatized and labeled."

An institution can also send a message to its employees regarding its attitude and commitment to underprepared students. Who does the college hire to teach developmental classes? How are they recognized or valued within the institution? Do they reflect the demographics of the population they teach? Roueche and Roueche (1999, p. 26) assert, "Dedicated teachers who want to teach remedial courses and who believe that at-risk students can learn and be successful… are the right instructors for the job." Adams and Huneycutt (McCabe & Day, 1998) state that developmental faculty should be "enthusiastic, dedicated and, most importantly, well trained" (p. 92).

The administration's attitude should be one that "respects the importance of developmental education on the campus and in the community" (McCabe & Day, 1998, p. 92) and welcomes underprepared students as they enter the academic community. Institutions that value remedial instruction, for example, commit funds to specially train faculty in adult learning. Faculty can become Developmental Education Specialists by attending the Kellogg Institute sponsored by the National Center for Developmental Education.

The status of remedial instructors also sends a campuswide message about the importance of the high-risk student. What percentage of developmental faculty members is part-time, compared with the faculty in other programs? Although research indicates that part-time faculty perform as well as full-time faculty in most disciplines, that is problematic in remedial programs where instructors need to completely understand the diversity of the at-risk population, have significant classroom experience, accommodate a variety of learning styles, and be cognizant of campuswide academic support services (Roueche & Roueche, 1999).

Organization

An institutional commitment to address underprepared students' nonacademic issues is evident in the placement of developmental education in its organizational structure. Most research supports a centralized developmental program or one that is well-coordinated and well-managed within the organization. Programs that place developmental courses within separate academic departments and under separate leaderships do not serve their students as successfully. Programs should have clearly stated philosophies and goals, included in departmental reviews and recognized in the institution's mission and benchmarks for success.

At some colleges, the developmental program may be part of a larger academic support effort. For instance, at Sandhills Community College in Pinehurst, NC, developmental education is included under the Department of Academic Support Services. This department, led by a director and an advisory committee, houses support for developmental students as well as college credit students. It includes special-needs advising, learning communities, peer and volunteer tutoring, and supplemental instruction. Serving high-risk students is central to the college's mission (McCabe & Day, 1998). At Delgado Community College in New Orleans, developmental education courses fit into the educational mission, which emphasizes that a DCC student will demonstrate proficiency in four vital academic areas, one of which is related to understanding the "social and individual behavior of human beings" (McCabe & Day, 1998). Thus, placement of remediation within the larger context of the college directly relates to institutional commitment and support of underprepared individuals.

Organizational structure must also include the muscle that some colleges put into their support of developmental education. This muscle generally connects to the value the institution places on preparing remedial students academically and socially. Roueche and Roueche (1999) discuss important measures administrators can take to strengthen the institution's commitment to developmental students. They include some of the following:

- Mandatory placement testing for all entering students
- Mandatory placement into developmental education courses based on assessment results
- Limited selection of academic courses that can be taken by developmental students
- Systematic evaluation of remedial programs
- Monetary commitment to support teaching and faculty development
- Increased support and structure offered to at-risk students
- Expanded pre-enrollment activities

- Strong support of good advising systems

- Required orientation

- Institutional support for collegewide attendance policies

- Limited course schedules for students who work

- Comprehensive financial aid programs

- Recruiting and hiring of the best faculty

- Innovative experiments in curriculum design

- Increased student services

- Completion of remedial courses as an institutional priority

These institutional commitments make higher education responsive not only to the academic needs of the students but also to their personal and social needs. According to McCabe and Day (1998), "Successful college-level remediation programs are concerned with the full personal development of students, hence the now-common term developmental education" (p. 19). In fact, many noninstructional components of programs for underprepared students relate to their eventual academic and social development. Some of these components include creative assessments and the building of working partnerships before, during, and after enrollment. Other noninstructional supports include collaborative activities, freshman seminars, and the making of meaningful connections with the academic environment.

Assessment and Student Placement

Students attempting to return to school after raising children or leaving the workplace often find testing daunting and sometimes damaging to their self-esteem. Still, we know that colleges must place students in learning environments that meet their academic, emotional, and social needs.

Community colleges, however, need to take into account multiple variables, increasing the probability of making accurate placement decisions (Morante, 1989). Some community colleges are taking the lead to offer more accurate and perhaps more humane ways to assess and place students. Some adaptive tests, such as COMPASS Diagnostics, are connected to refined assessment devices that highlight the needs of students and point them toward a full course, a specific module, or visits to a learning center (Tinto, 1998). (See a more complete discussion in Chapter 3, Assessment and Placement.)

Prince George's Community College in Largo, Maryland, and Santa Fe Community College in Gainesville, Florida, recognize that no single measure can unerringly determine a student's competency in a subject. Therefore, to assure appropriate course placement, both schools administer alternative testing during the first week of classes. This placement validation system helps both students and instructors (McCabe & Day, 1998). Other schools provide similar flexibility. Students at Sandhills Community College may schedule a placement retest or challenge a course by taking credit-by-exam through the tutoring center. Finally, some community colleges are exploring the idea of evaluating high school grades (e.g., a B or better in specified English and math courses) in combination with placement test scores to determine remedial placement.

Because cognitive and noncognitive development can complement each other, some community colleges are adding noncognitive tests to the student assessment portfolio. This allows institutions to evaluate the whole student. Many such instruments are on the market and some are quite useful in determining a student's learning style, personality, character, and temperament. These tests can signal retention problems and support needs prior to a student's first semester in college. The LASSI–Learning and Study Skills Inventory (H & H Publishing Company), The Student Retention Inventory (Noel-Levitz) and the Myers-Briggs Type Indicator are among the most widely used.

Daytona Beach Community College (FL) has implemented many of these creative initiatives. Student assessment and placement are expanded to include the development of a personal learning plan to guide the student through the first year of study (McCabe & Day, 1998). Although testing is still our best tool for placement into remedial courses, institutions should not rely too heavily on a single assessment measure. By designing a more humane process for placing a student, they can evaluate the entire person and better guarantee a successful college experience.

Building Partnerships

Institutions can further support high-risk students by partnering with others in the academic community. Internal partnerships include those important connections between instructor and students, curriculum and student support services, student and institution, and student and other students. These partnerships expand the community of support available to the underprepared individual.

To enhance readiness and ensure that fewer high school graduates need remediation, more and more secondary schools are partnering with local community colleges for pre-enrollment activities. The community college's close proximity to secondary institutions makes linkages with the public education system natural. The League for Innovation in the Community College has encouraged these collaborative efforts for many years (1990). These activities include administering the placement test as early as the 10th grade to give students enough time to improve their academic skills. For many high school students, early testing provides a reality check and an early warning that they are not following a path leading to postsecondary coursework. It also sends the message that placement testing is serious business. Too many high school students do not recognize the importance associated with placement testing and the connected ramifications of low scores.

Santa Fe Community College in Florida has assumed a strong leadership role in developing college-high school partnerships (McCabe & Day, 1998). Five years ago the college launched a project that included systematic testing and counseling for 10th graders and high school counselor workshops. The purpose was to provide feedback to students regarding their readiness to enter college in time for them to remediate deficiencies before graduating from high school. Over the past five years, SFCC has seen a 12 percent decrease in the number of high school graduates needing remediation.

Sandhills Community College has similar collaborative agreements with both of its area school systems. Besides giving placement tests before high school graduation, SCC also provides opportunities for high school teachers to take the placement test and attend workshops related to test taking and student anxiety. The college trains secondary teachers to offer placement-test prep courses for students who need remediation. Students may take these courses in a traditional class setting, in a self-paced learning lab, or online.

In addition, SCC recently forged a K-14 initiative with one of its service-area county school systems. According to SCC President John Dempsey, the partnership allows students to take their first college courses on their own high school campus, thus diminishing the anxiety often associated with meeting college professors. The association also increases dialogue between high school counselors and college advisors as well as high school instructors and college faculty.

By working closely with the school district, the college minimizes the paperwork shock that often accompanies first-time college enrollment (Dempsey, 2001). One interesting aspect of the K-14 initiative of the SCC Consortium is the Health Academy. Relying on a middle-college concept to get students involved early on campus, the project allows secondary students who are interested in health occupations to take both secondary and postsecondary courses simultaneously. At SCC, the Health Academy includes collaboration between the high school that provides advising, registration, and transportation; the college that provides courses and instructors; and the local hospital that provides mentors and physical space.

La Guardia Community College (NY), Miami-Dade Community College (FL), Cuyahoga Community College (OH), and many other institutions also have collaborative arrangements with secondary schools. As in most partnerships of this type, however, they serve relatively small numbers. We need to link partnerships involving higher education resources with the systematic efforts of the schools (Haycock, 1998). Internships and shadowing experiences, along with early testing, can bring secondary students into the life of the community college.

Additionally, educators need to construct a national framework that pays close attention to the role of the community college in school reform. The American Association of Community Colleges and community college presidents need to provide some supportive leadership. According to McCabe (1999), "Higher education can do nothing more important and more difficult than helping the underprepared achieve educational parity. Higher education leadership is essential in meeting this challenge. Colleges must join with the public schools in unified efforts to raise the education achievements of all children." (p. 8) In fact, it is in the best interests of community colleges themselves to ensure that school reform is effective and that students are able to perform in college-level courses upon graduation from high school.

Shared Responsibilities

Once the underprepared individual enters the campus community, the institution is morally and philosophically linked to that student. Vincent Tinto describes an effective partnership as one that retains students until they achieve their academic goals (Spann, 1990). First, the most effective institutions express an enduring commitment to their students. They continually ask how their actions further student welfare. All of the members of the institution–administrators, faculty, and staff–are part of this partnership. Student success is not the sole responsibility of one specific group: "Widespread commitment to students results in an identifiable climate of caring that permeates the life of the institution"

The most effective institutions express an enduring commitment to their students

(Spann, 1990, p. 19). Student and institution also work together to attain social and intellectual growth. Finally, the student-institution partnership is one of involvement and community. The college strives to "integrate individuals into the mainstream of the social and intellectual life of the institution and into the communities of people who make up that life. They consciously reach out and make contact with students in order to establish personal bonds...." (Spann, 1990, p. 19). The effects of student-college partnerships rely on the contacts students have with individuals in the institution, and the degree to which the students perceive themselves as active members of the college community. An embracing, committed partnership of student and institution is a nonacademic consideration that leads to student retention and success.

The student-faculty partnership is perhaps the most significant. According to Tinto, "One of the important elements affecting student persistence as well as intellectual and social development is the frequency of faculty contact outside the classroom" (Spann, 1990, p. 20). Astin's (1977) research indicates that "greater amounts of student-faculty interaction promote higher levels of student satisfaction with the college experience than any other involvement variable" he studied (Ender, Winston, & Miller, 1984, p. 10). What can an institution do to support this partnership? What leads faculty to make contact with students? What leads students to make contact with faculty?

Research suggests that faculty reach out to students when they perceive the partnership to be included in their instructional responsibility. If faculty members connect with just one student per day to express an academic or social concern, they can change the institution (Spann, 1990, p. 20). Instructors can spot the loners in a class. One incidence of meaningful contact with a teacher outside of class can help integrate an individual into the private community of the class. Administration can also foster the student-faculty partnership by providing incentives that make contacts feasible and simply by expecting faculty to make these contacts. In general, most students relate to those instructors who create a comfortable classroom atmosphere. Faculty who listen to students, who treat them with respect, and who exude a genuine liking for them usually form meaningful relationships with their students. "The classroom is the stimulus that makes people want to make contact after class" (Spann 1990, p. 20). Without a doubt, instructors have the most influence in shaping the classroom environment and thus have great power in making that environment a welcoming one for the underprepared student.

Another important noninstructional partnership that fosters growth in developmental students is the necessary relationship between academics and student services. Collaboration rather than separation best serves the missions of both areas. In many institutions, however, this partnership does not exist. Banta and Kuh (1998) discuss the importance of collaboration between these two facets of academic life, especially for underprepared students. Colleges must draw together as much information as possible regarding student learning and the changes that enhance it. Simply put, faculty and student services must share what they know about their students' in-class and out-of-class experiences. College-impact research clearly shows that "cognitive and affective development are inextricably intertwined and that curricular and out-of-class activities are not discrete, independent events; they affect one another (sometimes profoundly) in ways that often are not immediately obvious" (Banta & Kuh, 1998, p. 42).

Chicago State University provides an example of the benefits of this more holistic approach. The school interviewed students who did not persist. Most troubling, they found that nearly 80 percent of nonreturning freshmen surveyed indicated that they had no meaningful personal contact with any campus office, faculty or staff member, or student. In response, the university began a freshman seminar course that included collaboration with peers, as well as student services activities that encouraged student identification with the institution (Banta & Kuh, 1998). At Prince George's Community College, partnerships among developmental and college credit faculty and student support services promote a seamless transition from developmental to credit courses. For example, the institution has paired student services counselors and developmental instructional teams to provide interventions for developmental mathematics. Faculty members working with counselors conduct workshops, individual counseling, and classroom activities (McCabe & Day, 1998).

Engstom and Tinto offer a broad approach to address the nonacademic needs of students. They propose service-learning activities as a vehicle to combine academic and student support services to create socially responsible citizens and develop human beings. In their article, "Working Together for Service Learning," Engstom and Tinto (1997) highlight promising examples of faculty and student affairs partnerships that revolve around service-learning activities and make meaningful connections between academic content and real life experiences. Research indicates that one method to enhance the probability of developmental and first-year student persistence is to break down the boundaries of academic and student affairs (Spann, 1990).

Finally, peer support groups form invaluable partnerships for all students—especially developmental students who may have little identity with an academic environment. Former President of the Carnegie Foundation for the Advancement of Teaching Ernest Boyer observed, "I'm impressed that one of the most fundamental pathologies among the young people in our culture is their sense of disconnectedness–their feeling that they do not belong, they do not fit, and there is no defined purpose in their lives" (Boyer, 1992, p. 4). Underprepared students, who often come to college after raising a family, experiencing divorce, or losing a job, also have difficulty finding a peer group. Although the average age of the community college developmental student is on the rise, the reality is that older students may not have the time to seek peer partnerships that would lead to persisting through a degree. Research suggests that institutions that support communities of learners and collaborative learning opportunities–whether within a program, within developmental courses alone, or with developmental courses coupled with credit courses–create a climate conducive to human development and retention. Institutions, too, may provide opportunities for like individuals to meet. Clubs that involve individuals in student government activities, intramural sports, minority groups, and single parenting can provide the necessary opportunities for peers to gather–even in community colleges. It can be done. One community college formed a group for "sensible adults getting educated" (SAGE) that focused on encouraging older students in developmental courses to complete prerequisites, move into credit courses, and complete their degrees.

Learning Communities

Working partnerships are inherent in the term *collaboration*. One of the most significant collaborative activities that connects underprepared student learning with nonacademic concerns is the learning community. As defined by Gabelnick, MacGregor, Matthews, and Smith (1990), learning communities "purposefully restructure the curriculum to link together courses or coursework so that students find greater coherence in what they are learning as well as increased intellectual [and social] interaction with faculty and fellow students" (p. 5). According to Tinto, they form "environments of inclusion and success" for remedial students (Hankin, 1996, p. 13).

Learning communities began in the liberal arts curriculum, although because they provide support services to the underprepared, they now permeate developmental education programs. With both academic and social goals, they draw upon varying degrees of faculty collaboration, student collaboration, course integration, and student and physical support services.

The program at Holyoke Community College (MA) exemplifies such a community. The faculty may thematically combine a developmental reading and writing class with an introductory social science or humanities course. Learning communities may also form learning clusters in which developmental students take all of their courses together and build connections. The Evergreen State College's (WA) coordinated studies program and learning community efforts at North Seattle and Seattle Central Community Colleges are also of particular note.

According to Tinto, Russo, and Kadel-Taras, "Faculty collaboration in [these] learning communities may range from very little knowledge of what each other is doing to team teaching on a daily basis" (Hankin, 1996, p. 14). At Sandhills Community College, for example, developmental learning communities are a remedial option for approximately one-third of all underprepared students. A typical learning community at SCC consists of 20 to 25 students and three to four instructors or counselors who teach three to four courses from 8:00 a.m. to 1:00 p.m. These courses usually focus on a central theme, stress course integration, include college credit courses, and provide social and cultural development. Through integrated curriculum and extracurricular activities, students and instructors alike form learning partnerships that extend well beyond the classroom and course disciplines (McCabe & Day, 1998).

Research consistently indicates that learning communities positively affect the academic and nonacademic life of underprepared students. Tinto, Russo, and Kadel-Taras discuss nonacademic advantages of learning communities which contribute to the development of these human beings (Hankin 1996). (See Figure 4.1 on p. 59.)

FIGURE 4.1

NONACADEMIC ADVANTAGES OF LEARNING COMMUNITIES

- Students working together to build understanding and relationships which overcome the isolation they might otherwise feel

- Learning as a result of shared diversity of experience

- Enhancing student involvement by increasing social, emotional, and peer support from the learning community

- Students participating actively with their learning and their environment inside and outside of class

- Developing peer support groups and friendships that extend beyond the classroom and into subsequent academic sessions

- Creating a forum for students to address issues related to their own learning

- Building a supportive environment that validates student participation

- Creating a more positive view of the college, including other students, administrators, faculty, and support staff

- Increasing confidence in individual connections to an academic community, including the ability to use library resources and to contribute to the overall life of the college

- Increasing the motivation to stay in school and complete academic goals

- Nurturing the realization that a particular student is important to the welfare of a larger community of learners–educational citizenship

- Understanding diversity, shared knowing, and shared knowledge, which creates an inclusive environment supportive of minorities in postsecondary education

- Forming a natural bridge to connect remedial students to credit coursework

As in most endeavors, stumbling blocks arise when institutions implement learning communities. Initially, they may have to ignore traditional funding formulas that stress large classes, especially in liberal arts courses. There may be inadequate physical space to conduct learning-community seminars, or inadequate academic support services such as advising, counseling, and tutoring far from learning-community locations. Learning communities must have the leadership to coordinate advising, registration, and program activities. Faculty must accept the loss of autonomy inherent in a collaborative setting. Institutions must provide incentives for the increased workload associated with the curriculum development. Finally, organizational fatigue and the feeling of too much to do in too little time may sabotage well-intentioned efforts. In commuter colleges such as community colleges, underprepared students are at high risk. If they are to make lasting connections to the college, those connections most likely will occur in the classroom. Learning communities are an ideal method to address the nonacademic concerns of these students within the academic environment.

If high-risk students are to make lasting connections to the college, those connections most likely will occur in the classroom.

The Freshman Seminar

The student success course or freshman seminar provides another vehicle for a college to address nonacademic concerns of developmental students. Although in most postsecondary institutions this seminar is considered an academic course, much of its focus is on the noncognitive needs of underprepared students. According to Tinto (Spann, 1990), the freshman year should have a unique structure "based on the philosophy that assumes students develop differently in that year than in other years" (Spann, 1990, p. 24). Tinto also notes, "The first six months of college are the most critical in determining whether or not a student will become integrated into the academic and social communities of a college" (p. 52). In fact, nearly half of all beginning students leave college before the start of their second year. This is especially true of minority students attending predominantly White colleges.

During the first year and within the freshman orientation or seminar the boundaries between academics and student support should be broken down. The freshman-year experience should involve teachers getting together with other teachers, support staff, and counselors to talk about students. Colleges and universities have long used the freshman year to acclimate students to academic life; however, it is only recently that community college developmental programs have organized orientation courses for their students.

Community college underprepared students are likely to be the first generation of their family to attend college and therefore are often unfamiliar with its expectations and rewards (Upcraft & Gardner, 1989). Orientation courses that include college tours, learning-style inventories, diversity and motivation discussions, attitude and study-skills workshops, and introductions to academic support services help students adjust to the college environment. Discussions related to goal setting help high-risk students link their successes and failures to their own efforts (Alderman, 1990). Courses that emphasize critical thinking, match new students with second-year mentors, or partner with introductory credit programs have proven successful in improving performance, as indicated by grade point average of developmental students. In fact, research by Gardner (1998), reveals that underprepared students who successfully participate in orientation courses are more likely to be retained in the community college than students who do not participate in these courses.

Advising and Tutoring

In order to successfully address additional concerns related to the nonacademic needs of underprepared individuals, developmental programs must have strong advising and tutoring programs. These areas relate both to students' academic concerns and their affective needs.

Advising may take on an entirely different meaning for students and advisors. In fact, advisors themselves may have a vastly different view of the process. For some, advising is prescriptive, almost a clerical function. Students come to advisors with specific needs: course planning; drops, adds and withdrawals; and program concerns. Peripheral to any teaching, the advisor gives advice (prescription) and accepts responsibility for it. If the decision is a bad one, the student does not feel responsible. For some students, the advisor as an authority figure is a most comfortable role, especially for students of color who may correlate withholding advice to being untrustworthy.

More and more research, however, indicates deficiencies in this autocratic model and supports a more collaborative approach. According to Crookston (1994), advising is teaching. "Developmental counseling or advising helps the students become aware of their own changing self" within a rapidly changing society (p. 5). Advising is not only concerned with a student's course or vocational decisions, but also with facilitating an individual's "rational processes, environmental and interpersonal interactions, behavioral awareness, and problem-solving, decision-making and evaluation skills" (Crookston, 1994, p. 5).

In fact, the establishment of the advisor-advisee relationship and the fostering of the whole human being is developmental advising's first order of business. Together, student and advisor or mentor decide who takes the initiative, who takes the responsibility, and who supplies the knowledge. Both student and advisor learn through the developmental steps of this relationship.

Developmental advising does not always need to take a one-on-one role. Group advising and advising in freshman seminars or career courses can facilitate an individual's growth. To form a true foundation for advising excellence, an institution must view advising as vital to its mission and relate this commitment to all faculty; advisors must see forging personal relationships with students as central to their jobs, and students must consider advisors as partners in their academic and social development.

Fostering of the whole human being is the first order of business in developmental advising.

Quality advising for underprepared students consists of other characteristics as well. Quality advising is conducted by individuals who want to advise, and who consider advising an institutional tool for retention. They keep regular office hours, treat students with respect, connect them with appropriate campus resources, understand and recognize diversity, and periodically contact students during the semester simply to check in. Good advising, too, may include early-alert programs instituted by student services or campus advising centers to determine when students may be experiencing academic or personal difficulties. It may include programs geared to the special needs of academically deficient students, students of color, single parents, or other particular groups.

The Special Needs Advising Program (SNAP), for example, is part of the academic support program at Sandhills Community College. SNAP matches highly trained advisors with high-risk students. The college assigns any student who needs two or more developmental courses to an advisor who is a member of a team of developmental specialists. The

For underprepared students, tutoring is a vehicle of inclusion.

advisors work with the student until the required developmental courses are completed and then help transition the student into credit coursework. Typically, SNAP advisors will have their students in at least one class and will maintain close contact with them and their other instructors (McCabe & Day, 1998). This type of intrusive advising results in the most beneficial placement of underprepared students, as well as their increased retention and persistence. Astin (1993) concludes that the "student-faculty contact within any given institutional environment can have important positive implications for student development" (p. 384). Developmental and special needs advising are obvious ways to accomplish this contact.

By the 1990s, 73 percent of all colleges provided some type of organized tutoring program (Boylan, Bonham, & Bliss, 1994). Using a variety of tutoring methods is not simply a common component of remedial programs; it is a major factor in their success. Although geared to satisfy the academic concerns of all individuals, for underprepared students, tutoring is a vehicle of inclusion.

There are many nonacademic advantages related to tutoring when it is used to help the high-risk student. According to Hartman (1990), peer tutoring is a social process in which "the unequal status of the members of the cooperative dyad provides an opportunity for a social contract and developing social skills" (p. 2). This collaborative arrangement geared to a common goal is especially important for students who lack academic ability and somehow believe that the deficiency is their fault. Educationally and economically disadvantaged students tend to feel more relaxed with peers and relate to them in a more personal way, especially if they are enrolled in the same college (Maxwell, 1990). For this reason, Maxwell says, underprepared students who are tutored tend to remain in school longer than those who are not. Tutoring has also proven to have a positive effect on the attitudes and self-esteem of remedial students. Since academic performance is filled with emotion, student and tutor beliefs, motivations, and attitudes serve to facilitate or debilitate thinking and learning.

Many developmental students come to college with poor math skills and have a poor self-concept regarding their mathematical abilities. They blame themselves for being slow. This poor self-concept affects their ability to learn. Students with math anxiety have strong feelings of aversion and fear of failure. Tutors must access student's thoughts and feelings and help them to talk, analyze errors, respond to affective as well as cognitive needs, reassess the learning process, and then use real-life applications to cement learning (Gourgey, 1992).

Learning math, then, can become a vehicle for students to develop confidence in other learning skills. In most instances, underprepared students must voluntarily seek help in a challenging subject. When remedial students feel comfortable to actively seek assistance, they are empowered to take charge of their own learning, perhaps for the first time.

Although part-time peer tutors provide most tutoring, some colleges are now accommodating the underprepared individual's particular needs by offering a variety of tutorial support. Drop-in tutoring allows students of different levels to seek help whenever necessary without making a semester commitment. The sessions help developmental students accept tutoring as a natural academic support option for all college students. Computer-assisted tutoring and regularly scheduled open-lab sessions accommodate the developmental student with a varied work or home schedule. Flexible tutoring meets the changing demands of the student's life and accommodates a variety of learning styles.

Supplemental Instruction (SI) also proves to be excellent support for the underprepared student. SI emphasizes assistance for high-risk courses–those with a 30 percent or higher failure rate–rather than high-risk students. In this way, SI is open to all students in a course and it avoids the remedial stigma often associated with support programs. These courses also provide support groups for high-risk students who may not naturally seek such assistance. Within the context of a social group, developmental students find acceptance and the voice to discuss their own learning.

Volunteer tutors and mentors have been successful in addressing the academic as well as nonacademic needs of the underprepared student. Taking advantage of the local area's retirees and their interest in education, Sandhills Community College created the Generations Initiative, a program "based on the notion that close personal attention plays an important role in education, and that members of one generation have both the ability and the will to help with the education of another generation" (p. 3).

Sandhills recruited and trained over 70 retired volunteers to serve remedial students as personal tutors or as classroom assistants providing individual help in self-paced courses. Because of their efforts, in 1999 the college was able to assist more than 700 students (duplicated headcount) with developmental coursework and account for a higher than 70 percent pass rate among developmental students receiving tutoring assistance. Both students and volunteers reaped nonacademic rewards, and the effort continues today.

Tutoring not only serves the academic needs of underprepared students, it also helps them build community and confidence, build motivation, and improve their attitude toward learning.

The Whole Student

Each year, approximately 1.2 million students participate in community college remedial classes. A program designed for underprepared students, however, is not only about academics. It concerns the personal growth and development of human beings. To achieve this awesome task, community colleges must use all of their creative energies. They must provide strong institutional support and muscle to implement measures proven successful with the remedial population. They must find multiple assessment instruments that view the student holistically. They must build partnerships with secondary institutions and support a variety of student and academic linkages. Institutions must encourage curriculum development geared to addressing the nonacademic considerations of the underprepared. Advising and tutoring environments must be welcoming, flexible, and informative. According to McCabe and Day (1998):

> The greatest strength of our nation is the belief in the value of every human being and the commitment to help each person reach full potential. Perhaps more than any other institution, the community college holds the promise of democracy and the belief that individuals who lack important competencies do not necessarily lack the ability to fulfill personal educational goals. (p. 33)

5
CONNECTIONS AND DIRECTIONS

The most successful developmental programs reflect a strong institutional commitment that links the program with all areas of the college and to the outside community. The college demonstrates its promise to value and guide underprepared learners in their educational quests by working with offices and programs such as admissions, counseling, advising, records, registration, and general education. In addition, partnerships among the public school system and business and industry provide additional definition and relevance. All of these connections, both internal and external, help underprepared learners navigate their way through developmental coursework to credit coursework, graduation, transfer, and employment.

The most successful developmental programs reflect a strong institutional commitment that links the program with all areas of the college and to the outside community.

A joint report by the American Association for Higher Education, the American College Personnel Association, and the National Association for Student Personnel Administrators offers a useful guide for creating such connections. *Powerful Partnerships: A Shared Responsibility for Learning* (1998) maintains that the challenge of facilitating effective learning in the post industrial age is so great that everyone on campus must share in its responsibility. Community colleges face a substantial share of this challenge, working with underprepared students who make up a significant part of their population. No department can single-handedly meet the needs of these students.

The report further asserts that although we know a great deal about learning, we have not put our accumulated knowledge effectively to use. In community colleges, it has been typical for individual departments, rarely communicating with each other, to offer isolated instruction in developmental skill areas. A good case in point is the traditional separation of developmental reading and writing instruction that occurs despite the common cognitive base shared by the two disciplines. The complex needs of underprepared students can create a purpose for pulling together the best practices. "It is only by acting cooperatively in the context of common goals, as the most innovative institutions have done, that our accumulated understanding about learning is put to best use" (AAHE et al., 1998, p. 1).

A final justification for working cooperatively and in partnerships comes from the social nature of learning itself. The *Powerful Partnerships* report suggests in the first of 10 principles that

> learning is fundamentally about making and maintaining connections: biologically through neural networks; mentally among concepts, ideas, and meaning; and experimentally through interaction between the mind and the environment, self and other, generality and context, deliberation and action. (AAHE et al. 1998, p. 3)

Essentially, learning does not occur in isolation; it is a social process. As students learn, they interact with other students and faculty, and with the multiple perspectives of many disciplines. If community colleges are to effectively embrace the interconnectedness of all learning, they must actively model these principles in their organizational structures, policies, delivery of curricula, and support systems.

Organizational Structures

Traditionally, almost half of developmental education programs offered nationally have consisted of individual courses in reading, writing, and mathematics in individual departments (Boylan, Bonham, & Bliss, 1994). Institutions have justified this organizational structure with the argument that departments are able to provide seamless vertical connections to credit courses within the discipline. For example, when regular math faculty create and teach developmental math courses, it is easier to make provisions for curricular continuity to college-level math courses. Colleges that use this organizational arrangement believe that the departmental approach helps discipline-based faculty buy into developmental instruction.

When institutions take this approach, they sacrifice valuable connections. The departmental approach is based on an assumption that continuity to other courses in the same discipline is of paramount importance. In other words, the sole mission of a developmental math program is to prepare students for credit math, and the mission of a developmental writing course is to prepare students for English 101. In reality, however, developmental math, writing, and reading give students broad-based learning across the disciplines.

The departmental approach overlooks relationships to other parts of the institution that provide essential services.

Examples are endless. Students need basic math to better understand demographics presented in social science, to create an algorithm for a computer program, or to put accounting principles into action. Students need basic writing to craft summaries, article reviews, papers, and essay exams in all other subjects. And students need basic reading to comprehend all instructions, text chapters, literature, periodical articles, and reports. Furthermore, students need basic reading whenever they tackle basic writing and math.

The departmental approach to organization discourages curricular transfer and connection across the disciplines. It even overlooks important programmatic relationships to other parts of the institution that provide essential and interrelated services to underprepared students, including registration, advising, and institutional research.

A second and more successful approach to organizational structure is centralization. In the National Study of Developmental Education (Boylan, Bonham, & Bliss, 1994), students in integrated programs were more likely to have success in developmental English and be retained by the institution. The J. Sargeant Reynolds Community College Study of Effectiveness of Developmental Education (1995) also linked program effectiveness with a centralized structure.

In this approach, a single division takes responsibility for all developmental coursework, provides academic support, and collaborates with other offices. The centralized program follows Roueche's recommendation (1999) that institutions work with the developmental learner as a whole person rather than treating his various academic skill deficiencies in isolation. Boylan iterates this idea by asserting that good developmental education is student oriented rather than subject oriented (Boylan, 1999). By focusing on students, the centralized program endorses another learning principle put forward in the *Powerful Partnerships* report: "Learning is developmental, a cumulative process involving the whole person, relating past and present, integrating the new with the old, starting from but transcending personal concerns and interest" (AAHE et al., 1998, p. 6).

Other benefits arise from a centralized model. It creates an avenue for systematic advocacy for the underprepared student. When the developmental director or dean sits as an equal with representatives from other divisions for functions such as resource management and planning, the institution makes an important statement about the program's priority. In addition, program integration encourages ongoing monitoring of program outcomes (McCabe & Day, 1998). Most important, the faculty who teach in the centralized department are all committed to helping the development of underprepared students. The Community College of

The faculty who teach in centralized departments are all committed to the development of underprepared students.

Denver provides a good example of a community college that has achieved extraordinary success using the centralized model. According to Roueche, Ely, and Roueche (2001), a centralized model "helps prevent at-risk students from falling through academic cracks in the system and establishes a highly visible presence for the important role that developmental education plays in improving student success in the college" (p. 115).

In some older institutions with personnel or resource restraints, it is unlikely that departments can be completely restructured so that developmental coursework can be offered in a single division. In these colleges, faculty who teach both developmental and credit courses might be resistant to teaching only developmental courses. In addition, if an institution has a high percentage of developmental students, moving faculty who teach developmental courses to a new division would deplete the human resources of math and English departments. The creation of a separate developmental division might also further isolate developmental students rather than integrate them into college life.

In these situations, the highly coordinated program offers a third alternative. It can be established in two ways. First, a developmental division can borrow faculty members from existing English, math, and reading departments, giving teachers partial workloads in their home divisions as well as in the developmental studies division. This division can then augment the work of individual departments by providing additional academic support to learners, promoting the program to the college community, seeking external resources to fund initiatives, and evaluating and advertising outcomes.

A less desirable method for achieving a coordinated program is to create a committee that meets regularly and reports to a developmental education dean. The coordinating committee then has the responsibility for establishing policies, support systems, and programmatic outcomes research.

Regardless of what organizational structure an institution chooses, it is critical that the developmental program have a director or coordinator whose full concern is underprepared students and who actively advocates for them. This director must grasp the population's complexities, including cognitive and skill-based needs in reading, math, and writing; noncognitive needs in motivation, metacognition, goal-setting, career development, and study skills; social needs in collaborative learning, teamwork, and social development; and physical requirements in classroom and lab space, computer resources, and financial resources. Finally, the director also has to be able to establish the appropriate institutional connections and partnerships to meet these student needs.

Policies

As covered in more detail in Chapter 3, "Assessment and Placement", a comprehensive approach to developmental education requires policies regarding assessment, placement, and developmental prerequisites. Because students routinely overestimate their own skills (Hansen & Stephens, 2000) and are not familiar with the rigors of college (Morante, 1989), these policies must be mandatory to be effective (Boylan, Bliss, & Bonham, 1997; McCabe, 2001; Morante, 1989; Roueche, 1999).

But requiring assessment, placement, and developmental course prerequisites creates a ripple effect throughout the entire institution. Assessment instruments must first be selected if not mandated by the state; next, cut-off scores must be established with the input of faculty, again if not mandated by the state; third, a testing center must administer the tests; fourth, advisors must be trained to interpret the tests; and finally, the registration staff must carry out procedures to prevent students from registering unless they have documented placement results. Faculty of credit courses across the disciplines and those who design and teach developmental courses must communicate so that prerequisites can be established in a systematic way.

To be effective, policies must be determined and implemented through the collaborative work of many departments. All personnel with whom the student makes contact—including faculty, advisors, and admissions, testing center, and registration staff—must convey the mandatory nature of the policy to students in order for the institution to get across a single message about developmental education's importance. This single message will reflect the college's educational climate that, according to another learning principle in the *Powerful Partnerships* report, strongly affects learning.

> Learning is strongly affected by the educational climate in which it
> takes place: the settings and surroundings, the influence of others, and
> the values accorded to the life of the mind and to learning
> achievements. (AAHE et al., 1998, p. 8)

It is critical that in creating policy all stakeholders forge partnerships to build a consistent learning environment. But talking about partnerships is easier than forming them. When all stakeholders are brought together to voice different perspectives, legitimate concerns arise. Some of these concerns center around enrollment. Admissions officers and registration personnel, who pride themselves on the number of students they enroll may, for example, see a mandatory assessment and placement policy as a barrier to enrollment. Testing personnel may see the effects of test anxiety on student test performance. Advisors may see students becoming isolated if they are only allowed to register for developmental coursework. Developmental faculty may be more concerned about the effects of misplacement on their instruction than the students' total adjustment to the institution. Faculty across the disciplines may be concerned about the effect developmental course prerequisites have on upper-level course enrollment.

These multiple perspectives can thwart an institution's mission to serve its underprepared students. Nevertheless, by valuing the perspectives of all stakeholders, colleges will create a stronger program. In almost all cases the concerns are unfounded. Mandatory assessment and placement result in increased student success and retention, increasing enrollment at all levels in the college. Institutional leaders can help stakeholders move beyond their individual interests by determining whether a practice contributes to learning and how we know.

Mandatory assessment and placement results in increased student success and retention, increasing enrollment at all levels in the college.

The program director can then offer national research and local outcomes data to help make learning-based decisions.

Delivery of the Learning Program

Faculty who teach college-level courses and faculty who design and teach developmental courses must partner to validate the developmental curriculum (Boylan, 1999). By conducting literacy audits on all college-level courses, institutions can meet the ultimate learning needs of all students. The audit involves carefully analyzing reading, writing, critical-thinking, and mathematical tasks required in the college-level courses, and matching these tasks to the developmental curriculum. This will create college-credit course prerequisites that correspond to the skills students need. The developmental course competencies can then be matched to expectations. The systematic validation of the developmental curricula adds rationale for policies and for the appropriate sequencing of courses (McKusick, 1999).

Collaborative and innovative curricular delivery systems can provide solutions for many of the concerns expressed by stakeholders in the developmental education program. One effective delivery system is the developmental learning community. Developmental learning communities give faculty an opportunity to teach in an integrated and shared instructional environment while providing students with a chance to interact socially and collaboratively as they learn, thereby modeling teamwork in real-world situations. In one model, a developmental course is paired with a credit course. All of the developmental instruction takes place within the context of the content from the credit course. For example, developmental reading might be paired with Introduction to Psychology. Students would learn about main ideas, thesis statements, supporting details, transitional words and ideas, vocabulary in context, and other reading skills through direct application to the psychology text.

Because it enhances the ability of students to transfer what they have learned in developmental courses to other learning situations, such context-specific instruction is considered a best practice (McCabe & Day, 1998; Stahl, Simpson, & Hayes, 1992). This model exemplifies several of *Powerful Partnerships'* (AAHE et al., 1998) learning principles: learning is "grounded in particular contexts and individual experiences" (p. 11); learning is about "making and maintaining connections; and learning is enhanced by taking place in the context of a compelling situation that balances challenge and opportunity, stimulating and utilizing the brain's ability to conceptualize quickly and its capacity and need for contemplation and reflection upon experience" (p. 4).

Students respond to the developmental course when it is aligned with a credit course because they know that they must learn the basic skills to pass the credit course. In this situation, colleges could waive the developmental course's prerequisite because students would be receiving direct support in the developmental areas in the classroom of the credit course.

By requiring faculty who teach developmental courses to team with faculty who teach credit courses, developmental learning communities indirectly help refine, customize, and make the developmental curriculum relevant. The Community College of Baltimore County (MD) exemplifies such connections. In its model, a master learner–an advisor or a faculty member from outside the credit discipline–sits in the credit class with the developmental learners, models good learning behavior, and expands instruction by leading a seminar each week in which learning-to-learn techniques are discussed in the context of the discipline. This kind of discussion presents "learning as an active search for meaning by the learner–constructing knowledge rather than passively receiving it, shaping as well as being shaped by experiences" (AAHE et al., 1998, p. 5).

Developmental learning communities also help students form close relationships with each other because they share more learning time together. These close student relationships affirm the principle that "learning is done by individuals who are intrinsically tied to others as social beings" (AAHE et al., 1998, p. 7). Collaborative teaching and learning techniques such as peer editing sessions, think-pair-share activities, reciprocal teaching and learning activities, small and large group discussions, and multidimensional groups promote active involvement (Starks, 1994) and further expand the social nature of learning. The close relationships that students form with each other and with faculty contribute to the high retention rates that learning communities experience (Adams & Huneycutt, 1998; Tinto, 1997), helping to dispel some of the enrollment anxieties expressed by stakeholders in the program.

Supplemental Instruction (SI), an academic intervention developed and patented by the University of Missouri at Kansas City, is another successful delivery model used to assist students as they make the transition from developmental to credit courses. Directed by SI leaders, this academic enrichment program reaches students who have already successfully passed the high-risk course. The supplemental student-instructors enroll in the class a second time and model good student habits. They conduct sessions outside of class that focus on learning-to-learn and critical thinking through the course's content. A second form of SI, Video-based Supplemental Instruction

(VSI), uses lecture tapes that are later analyzed and discussed in VSI sessions.

Both forms of SI give students feedback, and offer them practice and opportunities to apply what they have learned—requirements for learning, according to the *Powerful Partnerships* report (AAHE et al., 1998). Students in SI sessions tend to bond together as learners and form affiliations with the supplemental student-instructor. Such relationships are important to student success and retention. National research on supplemental instruction shows that SI students earn higher course grades, withdraw less often, and have higher graduation rates than non-SI participants (Center for Supplemental Instruction, 2000).

All of these models share the close connection and alignment of the developmental curricula with college-level curricula. Underprepared students need to learn how to transfer the strategies they learn in developmental courses to the credit courses needed to achieve their educational goals. Stahl, Simpson, and Hayes (1992) suggest that institutions use a model for the delivery of developmental curricula that emphasizes transfer. Building such a model is dependent on a close partnership between developmental education and other disciplines.

In addition to collaborative relationships that connect the developmental curricula *up* to college-level curricula, developmental educators need to actively form connections *down* to high school curricula (McCabe, 2000; Roueche & Roueche, 1999). These partnerships often involve several steps. The assessment of high school sophomores or juniors with the college's placement test begins the process. High schools can use the test results to tailor their curriculum so that it adequately prepares students for the challenge of college. The results of the assessment can also be used by high school counselors in a variety of ways: (1) to provide additional basic skills instruction; (2) to advise students to enroll in sufficiently challenging courses; and (3) to identify students who may be ready for parallel enrollment in the community college.

Community colleges themselves can provide direct intervention to high school students through courses taught either on the college campus or at the high school. Often these developmental education courses are team-taught by community college faculty who pair up with high school instructors.

These pairings not only provide enrichment for students but influence future high school instruction. Such partnerships between community colleges and high schools, in place in many states including Florida and Maryland, have the potential to address the deficiencies of high school students who are at risk of becoming underprepared college students (Nunley & Gemberling, 1999).

A second type of external collaboration that gives definition to the developmental curriculum involves establishing relationships with business and industry. Frequently, these relationships come about as a result of the community college's occupational programs. Delores Perin (1999) argues that the infusion of basic skills into occupational instruction through learning communities and other partnerships makes developmental education more relevant to students, fosters student motivation, and ultimately increases student retention and success. Other kinds of partnerships between business providers of workplace literacy and developmental education programs form what Roueche has termed a "seamless web" with external agencies (p. 48).

Support Systems

Underprepared students require an array of support systems closely aligned with developmental policies and curricula. To be successful, these systems–which include tutoring, advising, orientation, and academic success courses–are built on a close relationship with other aspects of the developmental program. All of these supports help develop active and independent learning by emphasizing one particular *Powerful Partnerships* principle:

> Learning involves the ability of individuals to monitor their own learning, to understand how knowledge is acquired, to develop strategies for learning based on discerning their capacities and limitations, and to be aware of their own ways of knowing in approaching new bodies of knowledge and disciplinary frameworks. (AAHE et al., 1998, p. 12)

Tutoring

Tutoring is an essential part of the developmental program and contributes to student retention (Boylan, Bonham, & Bliss, 1994). As with developmental curricula, tutoring programs must be closely aligned to the full array of disciplines taught in the college. Learners must be confident that the skills they are taught through tutoring will be directly beneficial in the classroom. Tutoring programs can connect developmental students with paid student tutors who have passed courses in the subject they tutor. Most important, these students are trained in tutoring techniques. Research has shown that tutoring programs have an effect on student learning outcomes only when tutor training is provided (Boylan, Bliss, & Bonham, 1997).

To stay competitive and reach all students, community colleges must offer cybertutoring activities. Only developmental faculty, working in tandem with faculty from the disciplines being tutored, can build cybertutoring programs. Sinclair Community College (OH) has devised the Reading-Writing Connection, a cybertutorial created to address the learning needs of students in gateway courses such as Introduction to Allied Health. It leads the student through each chapter of the textbook, illuminating difficult vocabulary, highlighting important ideas, and building study and reading skills. In addition, the website contains valuable information and activities about grammar and composition. A faculty member in developmental reading serves as a cybertutor who answers the many questions posted on the site.

Advising

Researchers Boylan, Bliss, and Bonham identify advising as one of six critical developmental program components associated with student success (Boylan, Bliss, & Bonham, 1997). To be useful, the advising session must result in more than a list of courses in which students can enroll. At its best, an intensive advising program can help the underprepared student learn how to become a self-directed, independent learner. The developmental advising model is one in which the learner plays an active part in establishing goals, objectives, and a plan of action. The student and the advisor work collaboratively with other campus offices in creating an individualized learning plan. For example, to help a student better understand his own learning style and learning and study skills strategies, reading faculty may administer inventories which can be used in creating individualized learning plans. To establish career paths, the student can visit the college's career center and use various inventories that might provide information to help him match his own characteristics with those needed for a potential career ladder. The developmental student can also visit and interview faculty in the disciplines being researched. The advisor can then help him weave together strands of information obtained from these inventories and interviews and use them to build a plan which will eventually connect the student to faculty and staff in his desired major. Valencia Community College (FL) has created an exemplary developmental advising program using

Valencia's program has the added benefit of providing virtual advising, with plans created and then cyberstored for easy access by students and advisors.

individualized learning plans called LifeMap™. The program has the added benefit of providing virtual advising, with plans created and then cyberstored, making it easy for students and advisors to access information.

In another advising best practice, Community College of Denver (CO) uses Case Management Teams to lavish more time and attention on each student (Roueche, Ely, & Roueche, 2001, p. 94). In these teams, a case manager works with small groups of students to solve problems related to childcare, financial aid, and other barriers outside of academics. The program has been one of many factors in helping CCD achieve the distinction of closing the performance gap for minority students.

Academic Success Courses

A final student support service that can provide learning opportunities in the noncognitive areas such as motivation, metacognition, goal-setting, study skills, problem-solving, and critical thinking comes from academic success courses. Hodges and Dochen (2001) have provided a useful matrix for examining the variety of student success courses, which range from one-credit orientation courses to multicredit courses for learning-to-learn instruction and critical thinking. John Gardner of the University of South Carolina has been a leader in establishing Freshman Year Experience programs on two- and four-year campuses that contain academic success courses (Spann, 2000). These programs offer another opportunity for a collaborative institutional approach to serving the noncognitive needs of underprepared students. Student success courses are frequently taught by faculty and staff from all areas of the college, fostering an atmosphere of shared responsibility for addressing the needs of underprepared learners. When they are formulated as courses that address metacogntion and learning frameworks, they produce higher grades and retention (Hodges & Dochen, 2001).

In short, developmental education programs that partner with academic support systems build an environment where learning takes place not only in directed activities but

> informally and incidentally, beyond explicit teaching or the classroom, in casual contacts with faculty and staff, peers, campus life, active social and community involvements, and unplanned but fertile and complex situations. (AAHE et al., 1998, p. 10)

In the eyes of the underprepared learner, when the developmental education program partners with student services, the institution is transformed into a place where learning and opportunities for progress occur in every class, in every office, in every interchange.

Synergy

Attention to institutional relationships both from within and outside the institution can magnify the power of developmental education programs to address the needs of underprepared students. The president of Kingsborough Community College (NY), Byron McClenney, has asserted that community colleges cannot afford to sacrifice the synergy produced by linking together academic support programs (McClenney, 2000). Programs for underprepared learners simply cannot operate in isolation. These programs must actively and regularly partner with internal stakeholders from such diverse offices as admissions, registration, advising, enrollment, student life, and the entire array of academic disciplines. They must also create a seamless web of relationships with external educational agencies such as the public school system and business and industry. When developmental education programs create such powerful partnerships, institutions put learning first.

6
LEARNING AND CURRICULA

The National Association for Developmental Education (NADE) defines the purpose of developmental education as the ability "to develop in each learner the skills and attitudes necessary for the attainment of academic, career, and life goals" (NADE). Meeting these student needs requires an institutional effort. A single classroom instructor could not address the academic, career, and life goals of her students (Higbee, 2001). This triumvirate requires a coordinated effort by classroom instructors, counselors, advisors, and the students themselves. No single model has proven to be effective in delivering success strategies in all of the areas. While many exemplary programs do meet the trio of needs of their underprepared students, educators differ about the path to success.

In an interview, Hunter Boylan remarked, "The most successful [developmental] programs are theory-based. They don't just provide random intervention; they intervene according to the tenets of various theories of adult intellectual and personal development" (Chung, 2001, p. 19). With the great socioeconomic and geographic diversity among two-year colleges across the country, however, it is difficult to reach consensus on much of anything other than the fact that the population of underprepared students is growing. Chung says that developmental educators have not yet arrived at a viable theory to guide the discipline. He suggests three possible answers: the classical approach, the model-based approach, and the contextualist approach.

In the classical approach, educators of the underprepared would need to set out a list of laws that govern their discipline. In other words, if a student exhibited certain symptoms, that student would always be treated or taught in one manner, which should always be successful. The problem with this approach is that research has yet to indicate definitive answers to student learning problems.

The most common structure, the model-based approach, suggests that educators can construct a number of models "that accurately represent... student learning, success, failure, learning styles, temperament, self-concept, and so on." It asserts that we can assemble models from a variety of institutions, and that in individual cases the model may be effective. Educators can then arrive at the theory of a successful program. Longino states that the contextualist approach offers a broader foundation, seeing the remedial program in light of the larger society. "Knowledge, explanation, justification, and theorizing cannot adequately be understood unless we realize that all these things are intricately bound up with specific human and social contexts" (Chung 2001, p. 23).

In his seminal work, *A Learning College for the 21st Century*, Terry O'Banion offers his own perspective on the theoretical issue and lays out his vision for the future of higher education:

> It is possible for a college to flatten its organization, develop models of collaboration for faculty and administrators, develop processes for evaluating and reviewing its goals, and involve all stakeholders in learning how to do their job better and still retain all the same models of classrooms, lecturing, and teacher-as-sage as have been employed in past practice. (1997, p.100)

O'Banion further suggests that learning organizations are designed for the college staff, while learning colleges are designed for students. Spann notes, "Policy development without the input and continuing involvement of those persons who actually implement the policy is both demoralizing and dehumanizing. Serious and respectful dialogue between policymakers and policy implementers will help ensure the kind of policy that makes a qualitative difference in students' lives" (Spann, 2000, p. 22). Certainly, if such collaboration takes place, an institution has a much better chance of becoming learning centered.

Academic Goals

The academic goal of programs for underprepared students should be twofold: (1) to ensure that every student is prepared for the academic rigors of progressive courses in a particular content sequence and (2) to ensure that students are not allowed to enroll in a course in the sequence until they are prepared to be successful in that course. Programs for underprepared students must maintain academic standards and give students the competencies needed to succeed in college-level courses. Students are ill served by being passed from one level to another when educators know that they are not academically equipped for the progression.

Life Skills Goals

Educators must recognize, however, that not every underprepared student will be able to succeed in higher education. Many students will drop out of college before they achieve their academic goals or earn degrees or certificates. Programs for underprepared students must therefore have more short-term goals. Colleges can enhance the students' life skills by simply honing their basic abilities in reading, writing, mathematical computation, problem solving, and critical thinking. By improving these skills, students will be more successful in their lives.

Program Guidelines and Organization

Programs for the underprepared vary greatly across the country. Many are described as developmental education, basic skills education, preparatory education, or even remedial education. Often these programs are part of the college's academic unit, where an institution includes courses below the transfer level in the appropriate content field. The lower-level math courses, for example, would be part of the math department and the lower-level writing courses would be part of the English department. This decentralized organization allows for a great deal of communication between the lower-level and transfer-course faculty. It assumes that the individual departments are best able to determine the content of lower-level courses because they know best what is required of students in the upper-level courses. Other colleges offer a centralized program in which courses stand apart from offerings in math and English in the transfer areas. The centralized organization allows for coordination of course offerings across curricula. This is the model typically found in the most successful programs.

At other institutions, these programs for underprepared students are part of the student development division. By housing the program in student development, colleges can increase the emphasis on the affective components of learning. The strength of this organizational model rests with the ready access to counselors, advisors, and career development personnel.

Grading

Programs for underprepared students deal with grades in a number of ways. Many classroom instructors who support assigning the traditional grades *A* through *F* believe that students need to be rewarded for their efforts with good grades. Likewise, some faculty members feel that grades can motivate students, particularly in institutions that are committed to excellence. Other programs use competence as the foundation for their definition of success. If a student has attained what the program defines as competence in a course or in an individual skill area, then the student is assigned a *Pass* grade. Students who do not reach competence receive a *Fail* grade or, in some institutions, a grade that would reflect not only progress but also that achievement of required competencies is incomplete.

Other programs assign grades and also require students to pass a proficiency exam before certifying competency and allowing progress into the transfer curriculum.

With a growing political awareness about the educational preparation of this nation's students, some states have required students to pass a state-sanctioned standardized test before allowing them to progress into transfer curricula. Two examples of these state-mandated tests are in Florida and Texas.

Course Load

Most educators would agree that student learning depends on many factors, including motivation, background knowledge, home support, and commitment. Educators would also agree that students come to institutions of higher learning with personal, economic, and academic needs. To meet their needs, colleges must consider the decision-making process of the students.

At-risk students may not be academically prepared to enroll in the maximum number of credits allowed for a freshman. They would be better off enrolling with a lighter load and having a better chance to succeed. Students who are experiencing difficulty improve academic performance when their course load is reduced. Often, these same underprepared students take jobs that require a substantial commitment. They face the critical dilemma of choosing between being a full-time student and a part-time employee or being a full-time employee and a part-time student. Such decisions may determine students' success or failure.

Apart from this balance of work and school, some students' lack of academic preparation dictates less than the maximum full-time course load. Even with the most ideal schedule, underprepared students might yet require both academic and interpersonal intervention. Because of financial aid considerations, colleges often try to enroll students in a load that gives them full-time status. This is a disservice to students. It sets them up for failure.

Concurrent Enrollment

Educators continually discuss whether underprepared students should be allowed to enroll in college-level courses while they are still taking developmental education courses. One school of thought asserts that students should not enroll in college-level classes because they are not prepared to be successful in them. Unfortunately, it often takes a number of semesters of study before students can enroll in their first class for transfer or graduation credit. Some may get discouraged and drop out before that time. Other educators believe that underprepared students should be allowed to enroll in credit courses that have been preselected to give students the best chance for success.

A third philosophy suggests pairing content classes with remediation so students can build basic skills while taking college-level classes. Some studies suggest that these paired classes or learning communities can increase motivation and student persistence (Perin, 2001). Every student is different, and the area and depth of deficiencies vary widely. Students cannot simply be classified as developmental or academically ready. Only one in three underprepared students is deficient in all three basic areas. There are almost always courses for which the other developmental students are prepared. A student who is deeply deficient in all basic skills areas needs to concentrate on development of those competencies. Another student who has a moderate deficiency in mathematics should not be restricted from standard college courses that are not dependent on math skills.

Exit Criteria

Since programs for underprepared students vary a great deal from state to state and from college to college, there seems little consensus on what constitutes developmental program exit criteria. The most common exit criteria are still passing grades in developmental coursework. Some colleges have established competencies that students must meet. Others require students to pass an exit test before progressing to college-level courses. Some states have established standardized exit tests before allowing students to enroll in college-level coursework. Regardless of the criteria used, programs for the underprepared need to have clearly defined learning outcomes.

Other Considerations

Educators agree that small class size in most developmental courses increases individual attention to students and creates opportunities for more contact between faculty and students (Higbee, 2001). Some programs allow for open entry-open exit from developmental coursework, particularly if the program has an individualized option. This practice can work well if the course is entered and exited within a semester. Open-exit sometimes becomes problematic, however, when students require more time than the traditional 17-week semester.

PEDAGOGY

Educators should examine a variety of methods before deciding on a specific teaching technique. The most effective programs use more than one, and consider a teacher's personality, style, and training.

Lecture/Discussion

Lecture /discussion is the most common learning strategy used in college. Faculty are familiar with it, and it is the simplest for administration to organize. It is overused, however, particularly if it is a stand-alone offering.

Teachers who lecture provide students with needed information. Complex information cannot always be self-discovered. Since student engagement is often a critical need for developmental education students, discussion must accompany lectures. Students can be drawn into the presentation with instructor-initiated questions. Since lecture is still widely used in traditional college classes, modeling appropriate lecture interaction led by the teacher of developmental education courses is helpful for students. Instructors may assist students by providing background or a preview of the information to be covered in the lecture. They can emphasize important points and periodically question students or summarize as the material is unfolding. Finally, instructors can review the basics of the lecture material before concluding the session.

Certainly for some students, a developmental education sequence of classes may be very challenging. Much ground may have to be revisited to move underprepared students to a level where success is possible. Educators must organize the curriculum to provide a continuum. A course experience at any one level is related to and integrated with courses above and below that level. This would also suggest that curriculum developers get input—not just from the students, but also from instructors in college-level disciplines—to explain their course requirements.

It is important that the most effective instructional techniques and equipment be used to teach the course content. However, instructors should not base curriculum on any new media or equipment. They should design curriculum first and then determine what delivery systems and devices may be helpful.

Small Group/Collaboration

Students must begin to see that other students are a crucial source of help. Group learning, whether by formal collaborative plans, casual partnering, or small study groups, can show individual students how others learn. In such a setting, they may also discover new methods and attitudes. Motivation is often contagious. Students who cannot see the purpose or rewards of assigned coursework will benefit from students who are more committed to success.

Group cooperation is also a critical step toward life after school. Employers often require employees to share in goal setting, work, and completion. Whether the group study activity is a partner effort, an informal discussion group, or a collaborative learning situation, pre-group training is important.

Many educators feel that the ideal instructional situation exists when the teacher introduces skills or information to a class group as a whole. Then, the teacher conducts controlled practice, reteaches identified skills, and models appropriate learner behavior. Next, students move to small group or independent work and are ultimately tested on the material. Students who need additional help may be retaught, given more practice, and retested. The successful students continue with small group work, independent work, or both. Students may be encouraged to see the instructor or a tutor outside of class, or be asked or required to see a counselor to examine if any other behaviors are intruding on their learning.

Individualized

Some institutions use an individual instruction model. Logistically, such an approach creates more problems than the traditional whole class plan. Colleges employ labs to test students and provide individual learning plans. Students continue through a sequence of work, practice, drill, and tests. If they need help, teachers or tutors may provide additional support.

Many developmental educators question the sole use of independent instruction. If these students were effective independent learners, why have they not remediated themselves? Most students who are challenged by the basic academic requirements of reading, writing, and math benefit from structure. Though many individualized programs are structured in sequence, do developmental students have the knowledge or self-discipline to ask the appropriate questions? Do they complete the appropriate extra practice that may be required, or even use their study time wisely? As technology advances, individualized learning programs are becoming increasingly interactive. They are therefore becoming more effective for underprepared students. (For further discussion, see Chapter 7 "Technology.")

Teachers and peers are needed components in the instruction cycle. Some individualized independent work may be appropriate with specific conditions for completion. Time limits and working conditions–labs, computer log-in times, testing arrangements, method of reporting both problems and progress, consequences for falling behind, and accountability for seeking outside help—must be considered in the inclusion of individualized options.

This is not to argue against the considered use of individualized learning arrangements. They fit as a component of a learning program. College faculty need to keep open minds concerning the use of individualized learning programs.

COGNITIVE COMPONENTS
Reading

Some children enter elementary school severely underprepared. Without adequate listening comprehension, reading readiness, and family support for education, they start school with imposing challenges. Many will never catch up. Moats (2001) concludes that mature adult readers can improve if they learn basic reading skills skipped when they were younger and have frequent practice with important and applicable reading material.

Reading teachers realize that the ability to read requires thought. The ability to read well requires critical thinking. Paul Jewell (1996) defines critical thinking as "self-directed, self-disciplined, self-monitored, and self-corrective thinking. It presupposes assent to rigorous standards of excellence and mindful command of their use. It entails effective communication and problem solving abilities and a commitment to overcome our native egocentrism and sociocentrism" (p. 3).

Readers must retain concepts, remember general ideas, and be able to organize the material. The reader frames facts, details, and events into a meaningful arrangement. Throughout the process, students are asked to reach decisions based on evidence in the reading they think to be true. They need to make inferences about the unknown based on the known. The subtleties inherent in college reading material make it necessary for readers to interpret beyond the printed word.

The experienced reader understands that individual words themselves may hint at different suggested meanings. Monitored practice must guide underprepared readers to comprehend more than the obvious. Making sense of inferences is one of the most demanding thinking skills in the complex task of reading. The reader's understanding of a passage's main idea must, in a way, parallel the author's purpose and direction.

Writing

Mina Shaughnessy (1997) suggests in *Errors and Expectations* that in a typical 300-word essay, an average academic reader is likely to tolerate between five and six basic errors; in that same passage, the basic (underprepared) writers will make between 10 and 30 errors. If Shaughnessy is correct, then the difference between average and basic writers is merely a matter of error count. Any teacher of writing, whether basic or college level, knows that it is not the number of errors alone that differentiates and distinguishes writers (Ribble, 2001). An average writer may produce a paper that is grammatically correct, yet says very little. In contrast, some basic writers produce papers that, while full of sentence-level errors, are rich in language and meaning. Clearly, the number of errors alone does not define the writing quality.

Curricula for underprepared writers need to be multifaceted. Almost no writer produces perfect text in a first draft. In fact, there may be no such thing as a perfect text. While language is subjective, rules attempt to be objective. The juxtaposition of the two is sometimes messy. Teachers of basic writing might do well to teach their students to expect errors as part of the business of writing. Students need to recognize that the point of writing is communication. When students are afraid to write for fear of making an error, they will not communicate well. Teachers need to lead students through the land mines of errors so that they can concentrate on communicating ideas. When the ideas are on the paper or the computer screen, then the process of identifying and correcting errors can begin.

Mathematics

More students begin college less prepared in math than in any other area. The math expectations for beginning college students vary widely among states and colleges. There is debate as to the necessity of skills that are required in some institutions. Are all of the competencies essential to the success of all students?

Institutions struggle with student acceptance of poor math skills. Frequently, people even boast, "I can't get math!" Math faculty often assert that basic math courses help build competencies and critical thinking skills by requiring students to connect previously learned skills to the new concepts covered in class. Often in underprepared students' pasts, the ideas of numeracy and sequencing were misunderstood. First-level courses reintroduce and review these fundamental concepts. Problem-solving operations on whole numbers, equations, fractions, percents, ratios, and proportions may represent more of the content of many beginning developmental education math courses. New curricula in community colleges are focusing on additional real-life scenarios to demonstrate how basic math principles may be applied.

Computer Literacy

In today's information-laden world, what it means to be functionally literate has changed significantly. Spann (2000) lists reading, oral and written communication, computation, thinking, and problem solving as essential. Community college educators may want to add basic computer skills to the list of fundamental needs. The Internet and e-mail are two examples of the pervasiveness of technology in American life. In colleges, students face software-supplemented courses, online classes, library databases, required word processing, and calculators.

Study Skills

Frequently, experienced teachers of developmental education observe that some students simply have never been taught how to study. Cross (2001) suggests that students participate in class discussions on study habits, problems, and successes in order to share common concerns and ideas. Instructors can improve students' understanding of study by modeling the desired behavior or skill. Students can then attempt to work independently with teacher monitoring, encouragement, and evaluation. Finally, students must have opportunities to practice the new behavior. This continued practice ensures that students incorporate the new activity into their behavior.

Students must understand that to learn more effectively than they have in the past, they simply must change. Change in complex matters requires new attitudes, skills, critical thinking, committed involvement, and understanding. Examining student learning strategies usually begins with time management. A student's management of time goes beyond using calendars and writing priority lists. It also must encompass the ability to focus, stay on task, and use time efficiently. Underprepared students may look at the sheer amount of work that needs to be accomplished and stall. Some are paralyzed, fearful that even if they can make time to begin work, they may not succeed in doing the work well. These students require not only advice in maintaining schedules, but also modeling of this behavior. Instructors who explain the class session objectives and how much time should be spent on each one demonstrate an effective practice that can be used with independent study time. The teacher's oral monitoring of the total group's progress provides model behavior that can be copied by the students

The three mainstays of improved work are planning, seeking help, and learning from mistakes.

Instructors who teach beginning content levels of developmental programs must model effective study and work habits. Faculty cannot assume that students know the appropriate strategies. Rather than share long lists of advice and study skill rules with students, instructors must practice the three mainstays of improved work: planning, seeking help, and learning from mistakes.

Test Taking

Without a doubt, one of the most frequently cited deficiencies of underprepared students is in test taking. Students may often comment, "I just don't test well." Whether or not that is a legitimate observation, students must accept that a test in one form or another is a part of adult life. Work-related accreditation exams, tests as part of the job application process, and even driver's license exams are the norm.

The acquisition of test-taking skills is challenging. As part of a study skills curriculum, courses must teach methodic preparation and effective test-taking activities. Students must first learn the material and then convey this knowledge on the test. As part of their time management plan, students should carefully construct a study schedule. Underprepared students often underestimate the amount of study time necessary. They are shocked to hear that a study plan begins at the start of the term, not a week before the test.

Faculty must present the mandatory steps for test preparation. Students must prepare the study schedule and prioritize the course topics. They need to organize course materials such as textbooks, lecture notes, handouts, outlines, and study guides. The most neglected ideas as well as troubleshooting must be emphasized. Students must ask instructors for help, obtain tutoring, and plan study-group meetings to address the trouble they encounter in their test-prep strategy. Often, students spend unproductive hours looking at course material but never strategizing or practice-testing.

Study skill preparation must include creating practice tests. Rehearsing this process shows students why and how material appears on the test instrument. The final critical component for improved test taking is adaptability. Unforeseen events take place in everyone's life. Studying always requires more time than is scheduled. When students have problems with work schedules or childcare, they simply must account for alternative study time in their plans.

Many more specific test-taking skills, including understanding directions, timing, multiple choice and essay mastery, guessing, proofreading, and post-test analysis are frequently included in study skills classes.

Systematic and methodical planning may help tame test butterflies, but even when prepared, some students still battle test anxiety. Counseling staffs should conduct workshops or course visits addressing the physiological, emotional, or intellectual symptoms of this troublesome issue. If instructors demonstrate that tests are not punitive but instead show student success and accomplishment, students may adopt a positive attitude toward the process.

Note Taking

Many study skills curricula include detailed instruction on a variety of note-taking strategies. These are present because note taking requires students to improve thinking by using words to represent ideas learned from listening or reading. Students arrange these words in formal outlines, in formats such as the Cornell Method, in informal notes, in summaries, and in the more creative mapping techniques. As an added bonus, students are more actively involved when they clearly organize and determine hierarchies of material.

The current trend is to introduce students to the more creative, more visual mapping or linking systems. Other course designs still reinforce formal outlines because students may be required to construct them in traditional college-level coursework. Whether institutions use new or old systems, the goal remains the same: Students must learn to clearly express the ideas learned.

Strategies

Underprepared student programs also introduce reading, study plans, and strategies either in the study skills or reading curricula. Over the last 50 years, colleges have created a multitude of plans such as SQ3R, PQRST, RRR, and VCR3. Each of these strategies attempts to show students deliberate steps in studying and reading processes. They encourage students to focus on prereading, reading, and postreading activities and to condense and recollect important ideas. These study plans are critical to building effective study skills.

Literacy can be explained as minimal levels of reading and writing to succeed in everyday tasks. With the technology inherent in all walks of life, computer literacy may be the new frontier for underprepared students. Students must be aware of computerized assessment tests, publisher-maintained companion websites, e-mail, increasing use of the Internet for research, and online coursework. If the college mission is to prepare the underprepared, certainly institutions must spend some time on this new component of higher education.

AFFECTIVE COMPONENTS

Learning Styles Inventories

It would be a mistake to assume that the only problems underprepared students have with learning are in the cognitive realm. The concept of learner-centered education is that students need to make strong connections between the content and their perceptions about learning (Perin, 2001). Counselors, advisors, financial aid staff, and other student services personnel can do much to increase the effectiveness of communication between students and faculty (Higbee, 2001). In addition to helping students make the connections about their perceptions of learning, some institutions attempt to help students define their learning style. Learning style inventories, such as the LSI, the LASSI, the Dunn & Dunn Learning Style Model, the Productivity Environmental Preference Survey (PEPS), and the Myers Briggs, attempt in some way to characterize how students learn. If learning styles and teaching or dissemination styles can be identified, students have a better chance of choosing a delivery method that most closely aligns with their ability to learn. Some educators, however, feel that students need to be exposed to a range of teaching styles so that they can develop adaptive strategies that will allow them to be successful in any situation.

Learning Support

Study groups are a common element in almost any area of graduate education. Students in law school, medical school, and master's and doctoral programs know full well the benefit of pooling efforts to achieve individual success. Often, however, underprepared students mistakenly believe that learning is a solitary activity. They often need encouragement or even institutional assistance in organizing and conducting study groups. This assistance can prove beneficial for many students.

Tutors can contribute significantly to student progress, particularly progress of students enrolled in developmental education programs. When community colleges create tutoring programs, they must obtain guidance from department staff and instructors most knowledgeable about student needs. Institutions must take care when hiring tutors. Patience and organizational skills are as important as content mastery. Tutors should undergo mandatory, continuing training and be instructed in appropriate teaching methods and tutor-student interactions. Colleges should monitor tutor work and compatibility with students. Developmental education students should be encouraged, even required, to seek tutoring when needed.

Some institutions offer Supplemental Instruction (SI) as the only source of help to students challenged by coursework. Other community colleges combine the principles of SI with some of the components of learning communities by blocking students into groups. Individual group members may share the same deficiencies. The basic skill course attached to this plan would then supplement the student's other coursework. Institutions with some form of Supplemental Instruction can tailor the assignments and special assistance that students require.

Students with Learning Disabilities

Students with learning disabilities (LD) are attending community colleges in growing numbers every year. In the late 1980s, more than 130,000 students with learning disabilities attended college, and that number grew substantially in the 1990s (Matthews, Anderson, & Skolnick, 1987, quoted in Levison, 1996). The growth in LD enrollments is probably directly related to Section 504 of the 1973 Federal Disabilities Act. Community colleges are often the choice for these students because most community colleges have an open admissions policy and offer a more intimate setting than four-year institutions. In addition, the community college's proximity to the student's high school eases the transition to college (Levison, 1996).

LD students require services that are very different from those of other underprepared students.

Often, the learning-disabled student enters the community college as an underprepared student; however, these LD students require services that are very different services from those of other underprepared students. Community colleges must have programs in place to meet the specific needs of LD students. Such programs offer community colleges excellent opportunities for cross-divisional collaboration. Indeed, in many ways, LD programs can serve as a model for successful programs for the underprepared. Those services include but should not be limited to diagnostic testing, staffing to provide learning prescriptions for students, tutoring, developmental education in basic skills, and a coordination of accommodations for the student (Finn, 1999).

One important component is early communication between appropriate personnel at the high school and the community college. This communication can create a seamless transition from high school to college for the LD student. In addition, LD programs should have a testing and diagnosis component to identify or in some cases reaffirm a student's specific learning disability. Some learning-disabled students may be returning adults who have never had the benefit of appropriate diagnosis. For them, early referral and diagnostic testing is a necessary first step. After identifying student needs, staff from the student personnel and academic divisions of the college should meet to discuss appropriate programs and accommodations.

Olfiesh and McAffee (2000) identify five general categories that can be used to help decide service delivery items from larger psychoeducational evaluations for students with disabilities attending college: a summary of cognitive strengths and weaknesses, a summary of academic strengths and weaknesses, a summary of test scores, a summary of test behaviors, and recommendations for addressing the referral problems.

Students often find the following accommodations to be helpful to them and to their collegiate success: coursework accommodations such as note takers and books on tape, testing accommodations that include extended time and testing locations free from distractions, and access to LD staff. LD staff duties might include teaching LD students learning strategies and study skills specific to their disabilities, setting up peer study groups, reviewing student course schedules, and acting as liaisons between students and content teachers (Flynn, 1999). Most disability advocates, however, recommend that teaching faculty play a part in deciding accommodations offered to students with disabilities in their courses (Scott, 2000). Faculty development and training are necessary elements of a comprehensive plan for student success. Faculty buy-in and participation are essential to improving the learning of students with disabilities.

Many LD students take part in college classes without their peers or their professors having any knowledge of the students' learning problems. These students have successfully determined what strategies to employ in order to overcome their learning disabilities. Other LD students, however, require intervention by the institution to give them the best chance for success in college and in careers.

Disability Services

Students who received special education services in high schools and returning adults who may not have been diagnosed with learning problems often surface in the community college. Sometimes these students are reluctant to identify themselves as having learning problems. In addition, some seriously underprepared students enroll in classes at the community college because there are few options available to them after high school.

Colleges need a coordinated office of disability services to work with students who have learning or physical challenges that would impede their progress in college. The disability services programs can offer diagnostic testing and a coordination of services ranging from note takers to test proctors to specialized tutors. The extra programs level the playing field for these students. With proper assistance, many disabled students can become productive at the community college.

INTERVENTIONS
Academic Monitoring

Of all students entering the community college, undreprepared, at-risk students need to meet with counselors and advising staff to ensure they are making proper academic selections. In addition, these students should be monitored in their coursework. Underprepared students are often the least able to determine when they are in academic difficulty. They may have the false belief that they can pass muster at the last minute, despite the mathematical impossibility of resurrecting a 50 percent average to a passing 70 percent.

Some colleges have instituted collegewide academic monitoring or early warning systems to alert students who are having problems with attendance or academic progress, or both, early enough for interventions to be implemented. Early identification of students in academic distress is a collegewide necessity. Identification in itself, however, does little to help students salvage a course or a semester. Students need to meet with faculty or student development personnel, identify the source of the problem, and chart a plan of action to change the behaviors that are causing the problem.

Financial Aid

The source of some underprepared students' problems is a lack of finances. Students need money to go to school, so they secure part-time jobs. With their pay, they are able to enroll in college. To make the most out of their time in school and to get a degree as soon as possible, they enroll in as many courses as they can afford. They become caught, however, in the cycle of not having enough time to study for their classes because of their work schedules. If they reduce work hours, they no longer have enough money to attend college. Without objective advice from interested college personnel, these students feel trapped and powerless to improve their situations.

Other students find themselves in even more dire financial circumstances. They have no jobs and are only able to attend college because of financial aid. Because of processing requirements, financial aid often does not become available until a semester has already begun. Without available funds, students cannot enroll on time and they register late, which further weakens their chances for success in their courses. Other students may find themselves attending classes, but not having the financial resources to purchase the textbooks. Late enrollment and not owning a textbook almost guarantee failure. Financial aid intervention and even financial counseling needs to be provided to students so that financial decisions do not become obstacles to learning.

Recommendations

Institutions embarking on developing or restructuring their programs for underprepared students should consider the following as essential elements of the process:

- Institutions should seek input from practitioners on program design and guidelines.

- Institutions should set aside time for teacher planning and implementation of new coursework.

- Clear statements should identify expectations from goals and learning objectives.

- Institutions should implement ongoing faculty development to better enable all faculty to teach the underprepared student.

- Institutions should hire qualified full-time and adjunct teachers who express an interest in working with underprepared students.

- Institutions must ensure that all levels of coursework meet rigorous academic standards.

- Faculty should focus on the inclusion of active learning strategies into the curriculum.

- Faculty must conduct regular assessment within courses and programs.

- Institutions must conduct ongoing research–collecting and analyzing data–to evaluate and improve instruction.

- Institutions should be open to consideration of the use of technology in the underprepared student learning program.

- Programs for the underprepared should include intrusive monitoring and counseling to ensure the best chances for student success.

7
TECHNOLOGY

Rationale for Use of Technology

Given the increasingly pervasive role of technology in our daily living and working environments, the question regarding technology in education is far beyond whether or not. It is rather how, how much, and how best to use it. Technology can enable all

students to develop the competencies required for success in the educational arena and in the greater global, digital society. In addition to helping students acquire basic skills essential to using technology, its effective integration in the instructional process can help students develop the ability to learn independently, think about the state of their learning,

Technology can enable all students to develop the competencies required for success in the educational arena and in the greater global, digital society.

and alter their learning strategies to improve results. Technology coupled with sound practices on the part of staff can support these goals.

The use of technology in developmental programs boosts student success and serves to leverage the skills and contributions that faculty and staff bring to the learning partnership with the underprepared student. Data from recent literature (McCabe & Day, 1998; Boylan, 1999; Phillippe & Valiga, 2000) document the volume and nature of the current and future demands on community colleges in serving growing numbers of underprepared students. If colleges are to respond effectively, they must use both human and physical resources. Also, by integrating technology in developmental education, an institution can fulfill an important aspect of its mission. Examples of how technology can have a positive impact on mission fulfillment are listed in Figure 7.1 (p. 102).

FIGURE 7.1 POSITIVE IMPACT OF TECHNOLOGY ON MISSION FULFILLMENT

Extending Access to Instruction, Support Services and Resources

Combining on-campus participation with access through cable, Internet, or video systems

Providing options to begin the learning process when the need presents itself

Creating service delivery through use of telephony, radio, cable, public television, and the Internet

Responding to Diversity in Learner Needs, Abilities, and Situations

Responding to individual learning styles through multiple instruction modes

Responding to different rates of learning through flexible time frames

Effectively and Efficiently Using Resorces in Providing Instruction and Services

Using technology to complete tasks related to program management and student participation

Maximizing staff talents through unbundling tasks and using differential staffing in combination with support from technology

Extending the use of limited physical space by combining the delivery of multiple courses in the same facilities at the same time

Data from the annual Campus Computing Project surveys (Green, 2001) indicate that most institutions understand the need to incorporate technology into instruction and the business considerations of providing educational opportunities. The findings indicate the rapid growth in faculty and student use of PCs, websites, and Web-based resources and the increasing adoption of institutionwide commercial software systems, such as Datatel or PeopleSoft, that support multiple administrative service and instructional functions. Traditional videos delivered through public broadcasting or cable, radio, and point-to-point delivery of live or taped video have also changed the classroom. Indeed, the use of phrases such as distance learning, and terminology associated with it, no longer serve to make the same distinctions. Technology permeates the college campus.

Historically, community college faculty and staff have prided themselves on providing individual, personal attention believed to be essential to student success, particularly with underprepared students. To suggest that technology can and should play an important role in that process often engenders fear that this action would replace ongoing personal contact. But successful programs that make use of learning technology still provide a high level of personal interaction.

Although some of the existing literature suggests that students participating in remedial courses are very much like other community college students (Saxon & Boylan, 1999), some educators believe that these students are not only underprepared in terms of basic skills, but have had little or no access to technology and are intimidated and alienated by it. In fact, for many developmental students, the use of technology in the instructional process affords a fresh start, different from typical approaches associated with previous failures. Given the predictions for continued growth in the need for remediation, it will be even more important that colleges employ the very best use of both high-touch and high-tech strategies. This is particularly important when working with students who are beginning well behind the official starting blocks.

Tools and Keys

While audio- and video-based learning materials, along with computer-assisted instruction, have long been a part of many developmental education programs, the Internet, networking technology, and management software tools have all advanced the quality and variety of ways to support student learning. Computers no longer simply provide information or monitor practice and memorization of the drill-and-kill tradition. The advances are stunning, in terms of both what can be delivered and the methods of delivery.

The advances in learning technology are stunning, in terms of both what can be delivered and the methods of delivery.

Current hardware and software can manage the menial or repetitive tasks, and also seamlessly use sight, sound, graphics, and text to provide sophisticated educational programs. Multiple media has evolved into integrated multimedia. These programs actively engage the learner, provide opportunities for assimilating new information and practice, check for understanding, and support interactions with other learners, staff, or resources. Beyond their direct use in the instructional process, current software and hardware help deliver services and manage and track students–functions frequently required in developmental education programs. The use of intranets and Internet connectivity extends access, provides additional resources, and supports communication and collaborative learning activities.

Several elements are commonly associated with successful remedial programs in community colleges, for example:

- Flexibility in enrollment and completion options
- Assessment of skill levels prior to placement
- High degree of structure in courses
- Clearly defined objectives for each learning activity
- Use of mastery learning techniques
- Use of learning communities in instructional process
- Variety of methods and approaches responding to different learning rates and styles
- Provision for supplemental instruction resources
- Systems to document, monitor, and signal need for intervention
- Systematic program evaluation
  (Boylan, Bliss, & Bonham, 1997; McCabe & Day, 1998; Roueche & Roueche, 1999; McCabe, 2000)

Sophisticated, high-quality software and hardware coupled with a strong faculty and staff can do much to enhance student success in developmental education programs.

Content Software

Software systems may supplement other forms of instruction or provide the whole curriculum in a discipline area. While the degree of importance might vary with the particular use, good content software should include features such as:

- Well designed learning activities that are structured and sequenced to reflect sound pedagogy

- Pre-assessment activities to direct learning activities

- Clearly defined learning goals

- Manageable units of content

- Inclusion of a variety of media and tools for learning

- Active learning techniques such as simulations and application exercises

- Opportunities for practice

- Targeted feedback linked to learner responses

- Opportunities for learners to control time and pace of learning

- Assessment of skill or concept mastery
  (Checkering & Ehrmann, 1996; Tulloch & Sneed, 2000)

Learning Delivery and Management Software

Delivery and management systems offer many ways to effectively incorporate the good practices associated with excellence in undergraduate instruction. These may be purchased or developed to address one function such as e-mail or chat, they may be integrated into a specific content software program, or they may be platforms such as WebCT or Blackboard. These platforms contain a variety of features and tools used for communication, tracking, management, content organization, and presentation. They can be used with most homegrown or commercially produced course content material. Software programs can support faculty and staff through features that

- Provide uniform structure for course content

- Contain a variety of communications tools such as group and individual e-mail, live chat, and asynchronous discussion forums

- Provide tools for assessment of student learning

- Provide tracking and reporting functions related to student progress

- Provide group communication tools that may be used for collaboration as well as social interaction

PRACTICES LEADING TO EFFECTIVE USES

Technology has tremendous value both in helping underprepared students improve their basic skills and giving them competence to fully participate in the information society. If colleges are to achieve these goals and integrate technology into remedial efforts, it is essential that good practices associated with the how drive implementation and management.

The following guidelines should help faculty and staff to establish a sound basis for the successful use of technology.

Faculty and Staff Understanding of the Role and Potential Impact of Technology

- Provide faculty and staff opportunities to gain general understanding about different types of technology and how it can be employed in the delivery of instruction, services, and administration of institutional programs. They must see technology in action and develop an understanding of its value and limitations. To accomplish this, colleges should provide a variety of learning activities, such as conducting visits to other colleges, supporting conference attendance, presenting workshop sessions with expert users, or having vendor showcases. They should use in-house pioneers or colleagues from nearby institutions to serve as mentors in this effort. In the best scenario, this is part of a larger institutional plan.
- Address concerns of faculty and staff regarding staffing, workload, and compensation through clear policies and procedures.
- Provide targeted staff development opportunities that deal with broad issues related to the development and delivery of courses, such as intellectual property rights, copyright, identity security, electronic assessment of student work, and managing online communication with students.

Student Preparation

- Provide students with a series of activities that prepare them for their educational experience. These activities must focus on available technologies as well as the specific content, processes, and functions used in the software and hardware. This critical part of the process will have powerful impact on the program's success. Students need to know what will be expected of them as they use technology-based instruction and services as well as what they should expect from the technology.
- Construct the activities in discrete units so that they can be assembled to respond to the different experience and knowledge that students bring to the program. A unit on "netiquette," for example, deals with information and behaviors applicable to a variety of electronically-based activities, while the specifics of posting an assignment in a particular platform such as WebCT may have only limited application.

- Use the technology as part of the orientation process. While print materials are great for back up, they are no substitute for hands-on experience.
- Use the same principles in constructing orientation that are used in good developmental instruction. This includes providing bite-size units that use multiple media and active learning techniques, offering opportunities to apply concepts and information, checking for understanding, and assessing progress before moving on to other units.
- Provide orienting activities in an ongoing and flexible manner so that students who are unable to begin one course at a particular time can still acquire the essential skills for future opportunities.

Student Access and Support

- Know potential issues regarding access before integrating technology into the program. This includes information about underprepared students, including their access to computers and the Internet. It also means knowing the access the college is able to provide beyond class time, including number and location of lab stations and available hours.
- Expand instructional access to off-campus locations through partnerships with local high schools, the public library, or community centers. These types of alliances will serve the remedial program and may be the key to obtaining additional funding for computers as related to workforce development and other issues associated with access.
- Ensure that sufficient technical support for students in a variety of delivery methods is available.

Faculty and Staff for a Specific Implementation

- Plan orientation and staff development activities that incorporate the same good practices identified in the discussion of student orientation. (See Chapter 4, "Developing Human Beings".) As a result of participating in these activities, participants should be able to:
- Show knowledge about the intended purpose of the software or hardware being introduced. For example, if it is new course content software, what elements of the instructional process does it address? Is it supplemental or full-course? Is it an integrated program that is sequenced or are there separate units that may be used in a variety of ways? Is it linked with materials that are delivered through other means, such as print or video? What is the role of the faculty and staff in the instructional process vis-à-vis the software?
- Describe key roles in the instructional process using this program. Are faculty and staff roles clearly defined? Are they understood and accepted? Do individuals need additional skills or knowledge in order to carry out their roles?

- Evaluate the features of the software against the criteria for effective remediation and determine any actions that will increase the likelihood of student success. Does the software reflect the features of quality content outlined previously in this chapter? Does it respond to guidelines most commonly used by regional accrediting agencies as they evaluate instruction delivered electronically? (WICHE, 2001) What practices used in its implementation will increase student success?
- Evaluate the user-friendliness of the software in terms of navigation and support systems. Find out what kind of support the college and vendor will provide. Will it be 24/7? Is it delivered through a variety of means such as telephone, Web, or in person? Will students have access to the support or will it be exclusively for faculty and staff?
- Draft an outline of steps required to prepare for the course or other uses of the program. What steps need to be completed before students begin? Are the skills and information necessary for the tasks in place? Can students get additional help in preparation?

Beginning With the End in Mind

A significant characteristic of a successful developmental program is the use of a systematic evaluation process that funnels results into operations. To improve success, an effective program evaluation must include a statement of clear and measurable goals, specific information or data as evidence of goal achievement, and methods for collecting that information. For example, given overarching goals such as increasing enrollments, improving retention, expanding ability to serve diverse learners, or efficiently using institutional resources, how might staff evaluate the use of a particular technology-based instructional program?

Like other aspects of the program, the effective use of technology should be an integral part of the plan for addressing program goals. Because of the way in which most technology-based efforts were initiated in higher education, that is often still not the case. Historically, these efforts started as the result of the commitment of pioneers who were able to envision technology's contribution. The leadership of these pioneers and cheerleaders is critical in the beginning of a program. If the project is not integrated into the total program effort, it will continue to be viewed as an add-on or special project rather than an important part of achieving the institution's goals. Technology-based activities will be considered extra, and therefore subject to constant funding and resource challenges.

In tying the use of the technology directly to the program goals, it is important to formulate the questions that will be asked to determine its impact and goal attainment.

Examples of Evidence

The following sets of goals provide four fundamental examples of evidence that might be considered for broad categories of goals.

College Goal: Increase retention.
Evidence of attainment: Percentage of students who complete the semester, percentage of students who re-enroll for the next semester, and percentage of students who eventually earn degrees or certificates.
Program Goal: Provide more flexible access to developmental instruction.
Evidence of attainment: Use of instructional software program enables college to increase enrollment of full-time employed adult students. (Surveys indicate that 75 percent of developmental students enroll because of the flexible times for learning through the open lab.)

College Goal: Increase retention across the college by 5 percent.
Program Goal: Increase number of students completing developmental math Level 1 by a fixed percent.
Evidence of attainment: Number of students retained in the computer-based math Level 1 courses this semester increased by X percent. Is student attendance higher than in the same course the previous two terms?

College Goal: Increase enrollment.
Program goal: Provide remedial instruction that responds to different learning styles.
Evidence of attainment: Number of students with hearing impairments served this year through the introduction of instructional software in course.

College Goal: Increase the number of students served per semester in existing college labs.

Program Goal: Increase the student use of two labs dedicated to the developmental program.

Evidence of attainment: Use of instructional software permitted the scheduling of three different levels of English writing courses at the same time. Did the number of students served increase during the hours of 1-3 p.m.?

Beyond this type of data collection and analysis, in recent years colleges have been asking specific questions about the impact of a particular type of technology use on a particular transaction in the learning process. Beginning with FIPSE funding, the Flashlight project has continued to dedicate resources to assist colleges in designing studies about technology use in the teaching and learning process (Ehrmann, , 1997). The project provides institutions with expertise as well as processes for conducting studies to determine impact. In addition, it has created a database of questions to assist colleges in their building of research projects.

This kind of research is far more useful than comparing the relative merits of computer use in the instructional process with the traditional lecture and discussion classroom. In addition to the fact that such comparison has been fraught with difficulties–including the inability to control powerful variables such as the styles and behaviors of individual faculty–it seems unreasonable to try to equalize two very different methods of helping students learn. Determining the best uses of each method is a more productive approach.

8
HUMAN RESOURCES

Quality staffing of developmental education programs is of paramount importance. The educational task is particularly challenging. The underprepared student brings a history of school failure and a myriad of personal problems and needs. It is essential that our extensive knowledge of adult learning be used to full effect in creative program design. The staff must be comprised of strongly committed, well-prepared individuals with varied competencies and backgrounds.

Developmental education faces the challenge of meeting the needs of nontraditional students, high school dropouts, underprepared high school graduates, adults with diagnosed and undiagnosed learning and psychiatric disabilities, adults with social deficiencies, adults returning to college for retraining, single mothers, non-native-speaking students, and first-generation college students. With this population comes a range of skills and skill deficits. Faculty and staff hired to work with developmental students need qualifications and skills that extend beyond understanding scope and sequence, levels of instruction, forms of assessment, and forms of placement. Faculty and staff will also encounter underprepared students with personal, financial, legal, physical, attitudinal, and behavioral challenges that require resources and attention.

Developmental education faculty must have not only knowledge of levels of instruction, but also knowledge of effective strategies to meet an array of individual needs of adult learners that spans beyond the basic skills of reading, writing, and mathematics.

Selection of Faculty

Because of the range of skills and areas of expertise required, faculty need to be dedicated to teaching underprepared adult students. Against common practice, the majority of the faculty workload should be assigned to full-time faculty. These teachers must be in developmental programs by choice, not by involuntary assignment or as a stepping-stone to a higher level of instruction. Faculty can strengthen a developmental program when they have some combination of the following credentials:

- A master's degree in adult education, developmental education, elementary or secondary education, curriculum and instruction, special education, or ESL, with experience working with adult learners

- A master's degree with an endorsement, certificate, or experience in a specific discipline or specialty such as reading, mathematics, writing, bilingual education, ESL, adult education, learning disabilities, or educational diagnosis

- Experience in curriculum development, instructional design, determining a scope and sequence for the specific field of teaching and pedagogy, involving a variety of delivery systems or methods of instruction including the basic use of technology

- Training in the areas of learning theories, learning styles, learning disabilities, ESL, assessment, and cultural diversity

Employing well-prepared and committed faculty is critical to student and program success. Faculty who reflect the demographics of the student population not only contribute to diversity initiatives on campus, but also serve as role models for underprepared students and contribute to building their efficacy and success.

In the interview process at the Community College of Denver, applicants must exhibit understanding of their discipline or field, have a thorough knowledge of teaching methods and styles, and demonstrate that they know how to relate to students regardless of gender, ethnicity, or background. Regardless of the discipline, candidates are instructed to present a lesson plan that best demonstrates their teaching and learning philosophies. To assess philosophical parallels between words and actions, members of the interviewing team ask applicants to indicate how they would respond to a student scenario that is usually gender- or ethnically-related (Roueche, Ely, & Rouche, 2001).

Faculty and Staff Development

Not only should colleges recruit and hire the best-prepared faculty available, they should proceed to monitor, mentor, and train them in their cultures (Roueche, Ely, & Rouche, 2001). To realize the vision of a developmental education program designed to meet the needs of all students, resources must be provided for faculty and staff in-service development. These opportunities support a vision of teaching in which professional development activities are understood to be as vital to student learning as classroom instruction (NCRTL, 1994). An organized approach to staff development provides opportunities for faculty to stay current in the field of developmental education. As new research, new teaching techniques, innovative instructional delivery systems, and advanced technology emerge, the need for staff development grows.

As institutions shift from standards-centered to student-centered, faculty may also see a shift to student-centered pedagogy, that is, to the constructivist, active, or meaning-centered approaches that identify the particular interests, abilities, and purposes of students and use them as the basis for instruction (Grubb, 1998). Faculty now have a greater number of options for instructional organization and pedagogy, including cooperative teaching methods, collaborative instruction, independent study, supplementary instruction, linked courses, learning communities, computer-assisted instruction, distance learning, and online teaching.

Resources and training provided through staff development opportunities facilitate the learning process and acquisition of new skills for faculty and staff. Not only do individual faculty members benefit from training in new instructional approaches and new technology, they also benefit from the leadership that staff development programs can provide. Many instructional options, such as learning communities, distance learning, and computer assisted instruction, require a coordinated group vision and commitment of time, effort, and funding for support staff, equipment, and materials.

The movement of community colleges from teaching colleges to learning colleges is gaining momentum. It places even greater emphasis on the need for effective staff development programs. Terry O'Banion (2001) explains the philosophical shift: "A teaching college is not a learning college when the primary emphasis is on teaching–how to teach, when to teach, where to teach, methods of teaching–as opposed to a primary emphasis on learning. The question is not *What has been taught?* The question is *What has been learned?*" Felix Haynes, President of the Plant City Campus in Tampa (FL), distinguishes between a teaching college and a learning college:

> Since community colleges focus on teaching, it might be assumed that students are automatically learning. However, to truly be a learning college, an institution must focus on student learning. This requires assessment of student learning, an understanding of the diversity of human learning styles, and the development of myriad delivery modes. A transformation is required to move a teaching college to a learning college and it must be done through the hiring, development, and support of a faculty who are prepared to lead the students along the path of shared learning. (2001 AACC Internet Forum)

The Community College of Denver's Teaching/Learning Center, recipient of the 2000 Hesburgh Award for the most outstanding professional development program in higher education, serves as a model for effective staff development. The college makes sure faculty have multiple opportunities to fine tune their teaching skills, identify and implement appropriate instructional technologies, and stay current in their fields. CCD recognizes the critical role faculty and staff support services play in keeping instructors on the cutting edge of their profession. Established to offer quality professional development for faculty and staff and to further the institutional goal of improving student performance, the Teaching/Learning Center offers the following services (Roueche, Ely, & Roueche, 2001):

- Encourages learning-community and service-learning innovations

- Promotes valuing-diversity events and training

- Hosts 125 workshops annually, addressing faculty orientation and organizational culture; advising and retention strategies; teaching, learning, and classroom management techniques; curriculum development; technology; and diversity training

- Awards minigrants to faculty to pursue an innovative or creative project of benefit to CCD teaching and learning environment, with grant recipients sharing their project experiences and results with the college community through a series of workshops

- Develops reference materials on topics such as learning styles, diversity, electronic media, course content guides, academic Web-based resources, and online tutoring

- Trains instructors on the electronic media's versatility in course preparation, presentations, faculty-student communications, assessment, and grading

- Works directly with faculty to ensure quality online courses and support services

- Surveys faculty and staff for professional development and support needs, then creates new staff development opportunities to meet the college's changing environment

- Conducts periodic evaluations to ascertain whether or not it is meeting the needs of its community

- Leads the institution in its efforts to become a learning college

Additional professional development activities and support include the following:

- Funding to attend regional and national conferences, such as those sponsored by the College Reading and Learning Association (CRLA) and the National Association for Developmental Education (NADE)

- Membership in professional organizations, such as the American Association for Adult and Continuing Education (AAACE) and the American Educational Research Association (AERA)

- Subscriptions to professional publications such as *Journal of Developmental Education* and *Review of Research in Developmental Education*

- A meeting area where faculty can socialize, share ideas, and form reading or discussion groups

- Technical support to assist faculty in networking with developmental education instructors in other colleges across the nation and in locating and accessing educational research websites and resources

- Strategies to encourage and include part-time or adjunct faculty to participate in the array of professional development activities, services, and opportunities

- Communication bridges and training among different departments and services on campus, such as counseling, career planning, learning disabilities, library, student health, financial aid and scholarships, women's center, multicultural center, student services, and student organizations

Support Staff

Variable staffing is the backbone of most successful developmental education programs. These include program coordinators, trained tutors, peer mentors, paraprofessionals, lab assistants, computer technicians, counselors, and advisors. Together they provide the additional personalized attention and support that increases student retention and success, boosts confidence, enhances students' self-efficacy, and creates a sense of community. In addition to faculty, varied services provided by support staff are necessary to meet the needs of a diverse student population.

In addition to faculty, varied services provided by support staff are necessary to meet the needs of a diverse population.

In 1988, The Exxon Education Foundation awarded a major research grant to the National Center for Developmental Education to assess the efficacy of developmental education. The study became known as the National Study of Developmental Education. Through additional sources of funding, the research project continues today. One of the most important issues in this research is the study of the service components most commonly found in developmental programs. The six components linked to student success require different kinds of support staff (Boylan, Bliss, & Bonham, 1997):

- Presence of a centralized program organizational structure
- Presence of mandatory assessment
- Presence of mandatory placement of students
- Availability of tutor training
- Availability of advising services, counseling services, or both
- Presence of program evaluation

Support staff in developmental education programs are most frequently organized in a learning assistance program. Institutions use a wide range of names for centralized learning centers or support services programs (Sheets, 1998). Academic Learning Center, Academic Support Center, Academic Resource Center, Center for Learning Assistance, Learning Center, Learning Assistance Lab, Learning Enrichment Center, Learning Lab, Learning Resource Center, Student Resource Center–all these are common names for centralized support service programs. Regardless of title, they strive to meet the support service needs of all departments. They frequently house the tutoring services, study groups, computer-assisted tutorials, computer lab facilities, instructional videos, sample lecture notes, study skills resources, student-oriented workshops, and online resources. The centers employ one or more program directors or coordinators, learning lab and computer lab instructional assistants, computer technicians, clerical staff, tutors, and mentors.

Learning assistance programs provide student-centered learning programs and services for developing skills, strategies, and behaviors that increase the efficiency and effectiveness of the learning processes. By helping students achieve their learning potential and succeed academically, learning assistance programs significantly influence student retention.

In 1986, the American College Personnel Association (ACPA) drafted the *CAS Standards and Guidelines for Learning Assistance Programs*. These standards address the common aspects of quality learning assistance programs and articulate universal concepts, beliefs, and practices for these programs. The National Association for Developmental Education (NADE) and other associations sponsored standards development initiatives that culminated in the 1995 publication of the *NADE Self-Evaluation Guides: Models for Assessing Learning Assistance/Developmental Education Programs*. In the early 1990s, NADE, the College Reading and Learning Association (CRLA) and the CAS enterprise revised the *NADE Self-Evaluation Guides* and produced the *CAS Standards and Guidelines for Learning Assistance Programs* (Materniak, Maxwell, & Thayer, 1997).

CAS Standards and Guidelines for Learning Assistance Programs includes but is not limited to standards and guidelines for the mission, program, leadership, organization and management, human resources, financial resources, facilities, technology, and equipment for learning assistance programs (http://www.cas.edu). Standards and guidelines that specifically relate to staffing include the following:

- Institutions must appoint, position, and empower learning assistance program administrators within the administrative structure to accomplish stated missions. These administrators must be selected on the basis of formal education and training, relevant work experience, personal attributes, and other professional credentials.

- The program must establish procedures for staff selection, training, and evaluation.

- Staff and faculty must be committed to the mission, philosophy, goals, and priorities of the program and must possess the necessary expertise for assigned responsibilities.

- Professional staff members must hold an earned graduate degree in a field relevant to the learning assistance position and must possess an appropriate combination of education and experience.

- Learning assistance professionals should be knowledgeable in learning theory and in the instruction, assessment, theory, and professional standards of practice for their area of specialization and responsibility. They should understand the characteristics and needs of the populations they serve.

- Learning assistance program student employees and volunteers must be carefully selected, trained, supervised, and evaluated.

- The learning assistance program must have secretarial and technical staff adequate to accomplish its mission.

- The learning assistance program must employ a diverse staff to reflect the institution's student population, to ensure the existence of readily identifiable role models for students, and to enrich the campus community.

The Academic Support Center at the Community College of Denver is a model learning assistance program. The center provides a multicultural alternative learning environment that serves as a major retention resource by providing a point of unity and support for all college programs; assisting students in clarifying and attaining their academic goals; facilitating communication between students and faculty; teaching students how to study by focusing on each of their individual needs; giving students a sense of community and connection to the college; and acting as an entry point and learning and teaching environment for the students.

The center houses a reading and study skills lab, math lab, writing lab, online writing lab, online math educator, ESL, special learning support program for students with learning disabilities, student support services (a TRIO program), and vocational tutoring services. Services also include one-on-one tutoring, small group work, and computer-assisted learning. Staffing in this center includes full-time faculty with split assignments (part of the workload includes assigned lab time), tutors, technical support personnel, a computer-aided instruction specialist, and coordinators who are full-time faculty working split assignments (Roueche, Ely, & Roueche, 2001).

Tutors

Studies have shown that tutor training is essential for successful tutoring programs. The National Study of Developmental Education confirmed these findings. Tutoring programs with training components have a positive relationship to student GPA and retention. According to Boylan, Bonham, and Bliss (1994), 70 percent of the nation's tutorial programs have a training component.

In 1998, the CRLA initiated the Tutor Certification Program to establish minimum standards of skills and training for tutors. Their tutor training certification is used in over 300 college and university tutorial programs and is endorsed by NADE, Commission XVI of the American College Personnel Association, the American Council of Developmental Education Associations, and the National Tutoring Association (CRLA).

CRLA offers three levels of certification. Each level requires a minimum of 10 hours of tutor training and 25 hours of tutoring experience. Tutor coordinators or trainers receive guidelines for certification and choices of topics to include in their tutor training program. Typical topics include definition of tutoring, responsibilities, techniques, role modeling; goal-setting, communication skills, active listening and paraphrasing, referral skills, study skills, critical thinking and problem-solving skills, ethics and philosophy, using probing questions, characteristics of adult learners and learning styles, cultural awareness and intercultural communications, identifying and using resources, tutoring in specific skill or subject areas, record keeping, assertiveness training, and group management skills.

On many campuses with a CRLA tutor certification program, the tutoring coordinator or trainer presents a series of workshops or classes offered under a specific credit-bearing course. Tutors register for the course and receive college credit, which in turn generates FTE for the college. A variety of sources may be used to recruit tutors for the program:

- Students recommended by faculty
- Former students who have completed developmental courses and have previously received tutoring services
- Work-study and cooperative work experience students
- Undergraduate teacher education majors
- University graduate students
- Part-time or retired teachers
- Paraprofessionals and individuals from the community
- Retired professionals

The Learning Assistance Center (LAC) at San Francisco State University provides one model for tutoring programs. Faculty, graduate teaching assistants, and trained tutors work with students on course assignments across the disciplines. They also help students develop study skills necessary to succeed in college. Tutoring can be by appointment or on a drop-in basis. Students can schedule up to two 50-minute sessions per week with the same tutor.

Scheduled tutoring appointments are best for students who have many questions and want to develop their reading, writing, time-management, test-taking, problem-solving, and study skills. Scheduled appointments may involve one-on-one or study-group work. Drop-in sessions last 30 minutes and are available for students who need help on a specific problem or concept and need short-term support. Students can access a schedule of available tutors by subject on the university's website or at the LAC. In addition to working on course-specific content, tutors help students develop additional skills including:

- *Writing*: understanding assignments, planning and getting started, preparing research, citing sources, making revisions, editing, and proofreading
- *Reading*: planning reading schedules, reading textbooks effectively, locating main ideas, summarizing, comprehending, and retaining information
- *Math and Science*: identifying, comprehending, and learning to talk about concepts; discovering patterns; making connections in material; and problem solving
- *Study Skills*: time management, lecture note taking, organizing information, annotating and marking texts, test-taking strategies, and asking questions

Tutors at LAC enroll in training workshops that include topics such as motivating students, assessing writing skills, guiding students through the writing process, maximizing student participation, understanding different cognitive styles and learning modalities, incorporating study skills in every session, understanding the reading process, teaching active reading skills, and teaching students to use textbooks effectively (San Francisco State University, 2001).

The Community College of Denver requires students enrolled in developmental courses to complete a one-hour-a-week lab session and a one-on-one faculty, mentor, or tutor contact. Often, the lab setting provides a surrogate family environment, offering the nurturing support missing in many students' lives. Dialogue sessions frequently triggered by student stories conveyed through developmental writing assignments provide opportunities for open communication and problem solving. The Community College of Denver uses three levels of tutors:

- **Peer tutors** are students who have completed two or three college-level courses in the discipline to be tutored, have no tutoring experience, and have a recommendation from a content area instructor. Peer tutors require training and support from more experienced staff.

- **New professional tutors** have at least a bachelor's degree or the equivalent in their field. They have less than two years of teaching or tutoring experience. They receive training and support.

- **Professional tutors** have a minimum of a bachelor's degree or equivalent, and more than two years of teaching or tutoring experience. Professional tutors are able to mentor less-experienced tutors, solve problems, and work independently with students. They may be lead tutors who help with the daily operations in the labs.

Both peer tutors and new professional tutors attend general training sessions and workshops that provide an overview of the Academic Support Center, reinforce study skills to use with students, and train students on the use of computer-aided instruction (Roueche, Ely, & Rouche, 2001).

Peer Mentors

Informal and formal peer mentors can provide support services to enhance the learning experiences of underprepared students. Informal peer mentors are frequently former students who excelled in a specific course, demonstrated effective communication and motivational skills, had exemplary study skills, and wish to facilitate small group discussions and study groups for students currently enrolled in the course.

Faculty identify former students as potential peer mentors to work with individuals or small groups of students once or twice a week. The mentors may become work-study students or gain cooperative education credits. Faculty provide the peer mentors with study questions to discuss, the current reading and homework assignments, and suggested activities to facilitate small group discussions or study sessions. Mentoring sessions, which are voluntary, provide students with an opportunity to form a greater sense of community, to participate in a forum to discuss ideas or questions, and to form social bonds with other students. The mentors often increase students' self-efficacy by serving as role models who successfully completed the course.

Formal peer mentors receive structured training in peer mentoring. CRLA offers three levels of mentoring certification for students who have successfully completed a minimum of Level 1 tutor training and five hours of mentor training. Each level of mentor certification requires additional training and actual mentoring hours (CRLA).

Additional Staffing Needs

A program director, coordinators, lab assistants, computer technicians, and office staff contribute to the success of a comprehensive developmental program. The program director oversees all aspects of the program, elicits administrative support and funding for the program, provides leadership for the coordinators, and promotes a collaborative relationship between the program and other departments, programs, and services on campus.

Regardless of the organizational structure used in a developmental program, support personnel beyond instructors are integral components and contribute to program success in meeting the varying needs of the diverse population of developmental students.

Staff Commitment

Effective developmental faculty and staff gain personal satisfaction from the advances made by underprepared individuals. They are energized by student success. Strengthening staff commitment can occur through numerous avenues:

- Create a faculty mentoring program by matching new faculty with teachers experienced in the same subjects. The mentors serve as coaches not only on instruction but also on departmental and institutional policies and procedures. Meeting for a short time each week to discuss instructional materials, lesson plans, questions, or concerns builds a strong sense of commitment, inclusion, and teamwork.

- Establish occasional faculty meeting times devoted entirely to discussion and sharing of the developmental education program, including curriculum, classroom activities, teaching strategies, assessment tools, supplementary materials, or technology components. In this setting, individual instructors have the opportunity to share their talents, enthusiasm, expertise, and classroom experience with their colleagues for the common goal of strengthening the program and student success.

- Create instructional notebooks that serve as course guides for other instructors or newly hired faculty members. Course syllabi, outlines, lesson plans, overhead transparencies, classroom activities, examples of students' work, answer keys, and assessment tools can be readily available in an organized notebook for individual courses.

- Explore ways to include part-time or adjunct faculty in department meetings, discussions, and staff development opportunities. Examine communication channels to ensure they are kept abreast of departmental and institutional developments and decisions.

- Establish clear channels of communication with the tutoring coordinator, advisors, and counselors regarding the skill levels in courses, course content, and course expectations.

Staff Rewards

For many dedicated faculty and staff in developmental education programs, student success rates and individual student testimonials are the most important professional rewards. Other forms of rewards can provide recognition for faculty performance. Some examples follow.

- Create a department or program newsletter that shares best practices, success stories, professional awards, or accomplishments and serves as a forum for sharing information.

- Create a faculty-led journal, such as *The Community College Moment* at Lane Community College. The *Moment* is a forum for high-quality, progressive articles of interest to community college instructors, administrators, and staff. The publication reflects a new vision of scholarship at the intersection of academic, activist, and community interests (Lane Community College, 2001).

- Through a campuswide electronic or published newsletter, recognize and congratulate faculty and staff who receive awards, honors, or recognition from community groups or professional organizations, who assume leadership roles in community or professional organizations, and who experience other forms of accomplishments.

- Reward faculty and staff by supporting their interest in professional development activities, conferences, and presentations through funding professional development opportunities. Provide a forum for staff and faculty to share their experiences and knowledge upon completion of the professional development activities.

9
ENGLISH AS A SECOND LANGUAGE

Over the last 20 years, the influx of non-native speakers of English has transformed the community college. Each new census confirms what faculty and staff in open admissions colleges long ago discovered: The community college classroom is the point of entry for hundreds of non-native English speakers attempting to access postsecondary education. Their particular linguistic and cultural needs have forced administrators and faculty to reconsider the traditional curricular models that have served the underprepared student.

Historically, colleges that attempted to channel this population through developmental education programs designed for native speakers of English ultimately failed in providing these students access to higher education curricula. Institutions did not consider the complex factors involved in their successful matriculation. Their path to academic literacy differs from that of native speakers of English. Even among non-native speakers of English, there is great variation. Factors such as age and level of education in the first language can impact acquisition of the second language. Adults and children, for example, learn a second language at dramatically different rates. One size does not fit all.

Development of academic proficiency in a second language requires a comprehensive curriculum that integrates reading, writing, listening, speaking, and grammar. In addition, the curriculum must include the sociolinguistic aspects of language study. Traditional remedial education programs that focus on academic reading and personal writing are often too narrow in scope to provide the non-native speaker with linguistic tools needed to succeed in college-level courses. Both teacher and non-native student become frustrated, and a cycle of failure begins. A successful program must be comprehensive and involve both academic and student services, including systematic assessment, advisement, placement, and tracking.

In the 1980s, community colleges across the country began developing special courses designed to assist the diverse non-native student population. These early efforts borrowed from the developmental education model in which special sections of reading and writing targeted non-native English speakers. Some colleges, influenced by university-intensive English programs, began separate, traditional English as a Second Language (ESL) courses. They were the first step in meeting the linguistic needs of this population. Over the last two decades, educators have developed a number of new and promising models that reflect research in second-language acquisition and academic literacy. These models provide hope that access to higher education can be a realistic goal for this emerging population.

Demographic Information

Ten years ago, a college classroom might have had only one or two foreign students, whereas in some colleges today, 50 percent of the students may have origins from countries outside the U.S. For the first time in the 51 years since the Institute of International Education began collecting and publishing data on international students, the number of international students studying in U.S. institutions of higher education has surpassed half a million (IIE, 2000). In the 1999-2000 year, 514,723 international (non-immigrant) students were registered at U. S. higher education institutions, a 4.8 percent increase from the previous year. The growth in international student enrollments now represents 3.8 percent of all higher education enrollments.

Students come to the U.S. from six major areas of the world. More than 50 percent come from Asia, 15 percent come from Europe, 12 percent come from Latin America, 7 percent come from the Middle East, 6 percent come from Africa, and 6 percent come from North America and Oceania. In the year 2000, international student enrollment from China, Mexico, and Brazil grew faster than international enrollments in general (IIE, 2000).

While enrollments are growing dramatically at all higher education institutions, community college international enrollments have increased at the fastest rate. Between 1993 and 1999, they grew more than 40 percent, compared with a 14.4 percent growth at other types of institutions. Fueled by better administrative functions such as coordination among campus offices, interest by community colleges in internationalizing their campuses, availability of quality but low-cost education, and flexibility in scheduling course offerings, the escalation has been dramatic. Even though the above figures are impressive, they represent primarily international (non-immigrant) enrollment.

Many higher education institutions—and particularly community colleges—also have large populations of immigrant students who have come to the U.S. to live, work, raise families, and become part of the American Dream. The 2000 census report shows that more than 13.3 million immigrants came to the United States between 1990 and 2000. More than 30.5 million foreign-born Americans made up about 11 percent of the country's household population (*Dallas Morning News*, August 6, 2001).

Nearly one-fifth of America's school-age children speak a language other than English at home.

Nearly one-fifth of America's school-age children speak a language other than English at home. In Dallas, for example, nearly 33 percent of public school students are classified as limited English-proficient (*Dallas Morning News*, August 15, 2001). The sources of the immigrant population have changed over the last century from primarily European countries such as Austria-Hungary, Italy, United Kingdom, and Germany to countries such as Mexico, Philippines, Russia, Dominican Republic, and India. This change has meant that most immigrant students now come to the U.S. speaking a language other than English or an Indo-European language (*U.S. News & World Report*, August 6, 2001). Many immigrants are from third world countries and have had very limited schooling.

Colleges can accurately document their international students, relying on accurate visa records. Immigrants are harder to measure. Admissions forms offer few identifying markers for permanent residents, citizens, or refugees. But it is important to take into account this growing number of immigrant students, a number that may be higher than census figures suggest. These students are part of the projected doubling of the U.S. population by the year 2100, from 274 million to 571 million.

The growth will be sparked by as many as one million immigrants a year, mostly from Hispanic and Asian countries. Hispanics are expected to triple in number by 2050, from 31.4 million to 98.2 million. The Asian groups will grow even faster, from 10.9 million to 37.6 million (*Dallas Morning News*, January 13, 2000). According to Ignash (1992), "Recent trends in immigration and foreign student enrollments are placing a growing demand on community colleges for English as a Second Language instruction" (p. 1). The community college must be prepared to assist these international and immigrant students by providing specialized academic advisement, proficiency levels of ESL and English for Speakers of Other Languages (ESOL) courses, and student support services as students make the transition from ESOL into degree-track courses.

Classifications and Explanations of ESL/ESOL Populations

The most complex factors colleges must consider in dealing with non-native English speakers include residency status, educational background, language proficiency, and academic goals. Educators must assess and understand these four factors in order to properly advise, place, and instruct students.

RESIDENCY STATUS

Citizens

These are non-native English speakers who are either native-born or have become naturalized citizens; they remain an active part of their non-English speaking community and may still need ESL training. Because admissions forms characterize them as citizens, they may receive assessment designed for native speakers and a score that may not be indicative of their ability to succeed in college-level courses. Further, counselors may advise them to take developmental or remedial courses that are likely to be inappropriate for them.

Resident Aliens

These are immigrants including those who have a permanent (green card) or temporary, conditional residency status, such as refugees and evacuees. Their educational background may be underestimated, particularly if students do not have documentation showing their high school or college work. Institutions usually identify them for special non-native English testing. However, they may still take developmental or remedial courses if their scores are low and, like non-native English-speaking citizens, they may receive inappropriate instruction.

Nonresident Aliens

This category is for typical international students who come to the U.S. to study with intent to return to their home countries. They may also hold visas indicating special work or diplomatic status. These students must furnish numerous documents showing educational, financial, and health compliance in order to qualify for visas, and many have strong educational backgrounds in their home country. Of course, they may still lack English skills and require assistance from knowledgeable foreign student advisors. Assessment may include the Test of English as a Foreign Language (TOEFL, Educational Testing Service, Princeton, New Jersey) as well as specially designed placement tests for non-native English speakers. Many nonresident aliens enroll in approved intensive English programs since their status requires a full academic load each semester. If such a program is not available at a community college, these students may have to find a university or a private program to attend until their English proficiency is advanced enough for them to enter degree-track courses.

Undocumented Aliens

The term refers to people who live, work, or study in the U.S., but who do not have official residency status. Their English skills can vary greatly, ranging from completely proficient to needing several semesters of ESL or ESOL training. Students in this category may be the most underserved. Even if they have been to U.S. high schools, performed well, and graduated, they may not be able to attend public institutions of higher education because of their undocumented status. In order to enroll, many must apply as foreign exchange students or as nonresident aliens and pay as much as three times the tuition as resident students.

EDUCATIONAL LEVELS

Students in each of the residency groups may fall into any of the following educational levels:

Students Educated in the United States

Some non-native English-speaking students may have been partially or wholly educated in the U.S. school system. The students may or may not need ESL or ESOL training when they enter higher education institutions. Often their near-native oral proficiency does not match their literacy skills in the language areas of reading and writing. They may still need ESL or ESOL training.

High-Level First-Language Educated Students

Some non-native English-speaking students have attained a high level of education in their native language. They have the equivalent of a high school diploma, and some may even have a college degree from their home country. Sometimes, because of their limited English proficiency, colleges place them in ESL or ESOL levels that are too low. Their ability to learn complex subject matter and persist to completion of a degree may permit them to move through second-language acquisition at a faster pace than others with the same level of English proficiency.

Interrupted or Low-Level Education in First Language

These students may have started their education but, because of economic or political situations, had to stop attending school. Even if they resumed schooling after sporadic attendance, they have many gaps in their educational foundation. When they come to a U.S. college or university, they may not have schema on which to build new information and may not have developed learning strategies that could transfer to ESL or ESOL and degree-track courses. The students in this category typically have to overcome the greatest challenges in the college environment.

LANGUAGE PROFICIENCY AND ACADEMIC GOALS

After a college addresses residency and proficiency issues, it must also deal with students' other academic and social needs.

Preliteracy Level

An increasing number of students come from third world countries, have little or no schooling, and may not be able to read and write in their native language. When they learn English as a second language, they must also learn sound-symbol relationships and basic reading and writing skills. They should be placed in preliterate, beginning-level classes with other students of similar skill backgrounds.

False Beginning Level

Some of these students may appear to have oral proficiency in English, yet they do not understand the language structure. They may even be at a preliterate level. Others may have a good understanding of the written language, yet be unable to understand or orally produce English sentences. These students present a placement challenge. Since some of their skills are higher than those of beginning students, they may be bored in a basic class. Some of their skills, however, might truly be at a beginning level. When possible, these students should be placed in proficiency-specific classes to bring their lower skills to the level of their higher skills.

Beginning Level

At this level, English proficiency ranges from none to minimal in the skill areas of listening, speaking, reading, and writing. These students, however, should be placed in classes that assume literacy in their first language (see preliteracy beginning level). It is important for advisors and teachers not to underestimate the students' intellectual ability simply because they do not have English proficiency.

Intermediate Level

Intermediate students possess English proficiency that ranges from basic understanding and production to an ability to function in the English-speaking environment. They must be challenged to expand vocabulary and develop more complex language structures, avoiding simplified or incorrect language patterns.

Advanced Level

Students assessed at this level usually function well in an English environment but need skill refinement in order to succeed in college-level coursework or in a professional work setting. They are ready to analyze grammar rules and perform simple comparative analysis of linguistic structures. They are also at a level of proficiency where they can use English to solve problems, propose initiatives, and create lyrical poetry and prose. These students should be challenged to expand their English skills in all areas.

SPECIAL NEEDS

Although this is not a proficiency-level category, colleges and universities need to consider elements such as learning disabilities, physical challenges, and psychological needs when they examine non-native English speakers' education and proficiency levels.

ESL/ESOL and Developmental Education

Non-native speakers of English should be assessed with tests designed for or normed with non-native English speakers. If students are properly assessed, they will more likely be placed in classes specifically designed for them, such as ESL/ESOL classes that focus on language acquisition rather than remedial needs, and that take into account students' linguistic and cultural backgrounds.

Second-language learning is an additive ability, not a relearning, a repairing of learning, or a mastering of concepts not gained in the first 12 years of U.S. public education. As noted by Mike Rose in *The Language of Exclusion: Writing Instruction at the University* (1985), remediation means that the student's academic ability is substandard or inadequate, with the implication that the material being studied should have been learned during prior education but was not. The learning of English in an ESL/ESOL program at a college is no different from the learning of Japanese, Spanish, German, or Chinese in the foreign language department. These are all cases of students becoming multilingual, but nowhere is it implied that the learner is academically inadequate. Second-language students need more language assistance, but they do not have any less academic writing ability. Studies show that essays written by ESL program completers and native English speakers exhibit no difference in scores as evaluated by English and ESL faculty (Brown, 1991).

Non-native English speakers need to learn English in specialized language-acquisition settings. Those placed into typical developmental education classes designed for native English speakers usually do not receive the kind of instruction or curriculum they need in order to progress easily and quickly into college-level classes. Further, they become frustrated by the lack of sophistication of assignments in a remedial class since, although having limited English skills, they likely have advanced thinking and reasoning skills.

Some colleges still do not have specific ESL/ESOL courses. If a college has no ESL/ESOL program and needs to meet the college-preparatory needs of its non-native English speaking population, special sections of developmental education can be designated for these students as long as specific curriculum is provided along with instructors trained in Teaching English as a Second Language (TESL). What is most important is that non-native English speakers not be placed in typical developmental education classes where the objective of the class would then have to become a mix of remediation and language acquisition. This complex mixture of objectives and methodology can easily confuse student populations and diminish student success–results that poorly serve both the native and non-native English speaker.

Current Research on the Status of ESL/ESOL in the U.S.

For many non-native speakers of English, language proficiency remains one of the most critical factors in the ability to access the community college curriculum. Over the last 20 years, community colleges have responded with a phenomenal growth of classes with the nomenclature ESL or ESOL. A 1991 Center for the Study of Community Colleges (CSCC) report sponsored by the National Center for Academic Achievement and Transfer found a 15.3 percent increase in foreign languages as part of the total humanities curriculum between 1977 and 1991 (Ignash, 1992). This increase can be attributed directly to the development of ESL or ESOL courses. In 1983, ESL grew from 30 percent of all foreign-language courses to 51 percent in 1991, enrolling 236,000 of the total 460,700 foreign-language students that year (Ignash, 1992). A study tracking ESL enrollment from 1991 to 1998 found a 38 percent increase in the ESL course offerings in the community college, confirming that ESL is one of the fastest growing programs in the community college (Kuo, 2000).

Size and geography are the two critical factors in the development of the community college ESL curriculum. Environmental scanning prior to the implementation of ESL programs has provided colleges with data on service-area immigrant and international communities. While present throughout the country, the populations that require ESL are concentrated in urban areas. Stiplin (2000) found that of the larger community colleges with enrollments that exceeded 6,141, more than half offered 20 or more ESL courses. The Western, Midwestern, and Middle Atlantic states accounted for 71 percent of the total ESL courses offered (Stiplin). Texas and Michigan are two examples of this phenomenal growth. Dallas County Community College's ESL offerings grew from 13 sections in fall 1985 to 705 sections in fall 2001. Oakland Community College in Michigan has seen its program develop from 20 sections in fall 1994 to 100 in fall 2001. ESL is the largest department at Miami-Dade Community College.

Community college ESL programs typically consist of academic credit courses, noncredit courses, or a combination of both. The programs are leveled by proficiency-preliterate or false beginning, beginning, intermediate, and advanced. Credit curricula, housed in academic departments (e.g., humanities or English), are often modeled on English for Academic Purposes (EAP) programs, in which the focus is on the academic needs of college-bound students. The listening comprehension classes, for example, concentrate on the listening strategies and note-taking skills necessary for accessing a variety of interdisciplinary lectures. The credit model includes ESL courses offered for institutional credit (in which courses are nontransferable but can often be used for financial aid purposes) and for transferable credit. The transferable credit option allows colleges and universities to accept ESL foreign-language or humanities credit. The student is acquiring a new language, not simply remediating an aspect of English proficiency—an important distinction. Despite this critical difference, only 27 percent of community colleges offer a combination of ESL course types that include transferable and nontransferable ESL courses (Kuo, 1999).

Larger ESL programs tend to offer bridge classes to college-level courses. These courses are attempts to successfully mainstream the ESL student into the college curricula through sheltered classes (e.g., Sheltered English or special sections of freshman composition identified for non-native speakers of English) or paired courses (e.g., an ESL reading course paired with American History). Continuing education divisions or community service departments typically offer noncredit courses that are often multileveled, integrative, and geared toward communicative competence. They emphasize the language needs for social and professional interactions.

In addition to credit and noncredit structures, many community colleges contract with local industry to provide either credit or noncredit English courses in the workplace and customized language courses that focus on the linguistic and sociolinguistic demands of the workplace. The range of delivery options and flexibility of course scheduling are often tied to the size of the community college. Not surprisingly, Kuo (1999) found that larger community colleges offered more variety and flexibility. Comprehensive ESL programs must include the support services of assessment, advisement, counseling, tutoring, and tracking.

Like developmental students, non-native speakers of English must learn to negotiate through an unknown and unfamiliar system. The application, assessment, advisement, and placement process can be daunting for someone who may have only recently entered the country. Many community colleges have created special advising centers to assist this population. Richland College (Dallas County Community College District) established the Multicultural Center in 1990, in part to respond to the changing demographics of its service area. During the 2000-2001 academic year, the Center advised 1,800 students each month.

Along with special advising centers, many community college ESL programs offer separate assessment for non-native English speakers. Historically, institutions evaluated these students with instruments normed for native speakers of English. The low-performing students would sometimes be routed to special programs for students with learning disabilities. With the emergence of ESL classes, however, appropriate assessment can measure second-language proficiency. Such instruments as the Michigan Test of English Language Proficiency (MTELP, The University of Michigan Press), the Test of English as a Foreign Language (TOEFL, Educational Testing Service), and newly developed computer-adaptive ESL tests are some of the instruments being used.

Specialized tutoring for ESL students in both ESL and non-ESL classes is just as important as advising and assessment. The Orchard Ridge Campus of Oakland Community College in Michigan, for example, has implemented Supplemental Instruction (SI) in the ESL program. Former ESL students serve as mentors and facilitators for current students. They sit in an ESL class, take notes, and then assist after-class study groups.

Ultimately, the test of any program is whether it produces results. Do the expenditure of dollars on staff and the allocation of space result in more successful students? The literature on outcomes with ESL programs at community colleges is spotty, perhaps because of the recency of ESL programs. A study by Richland College's Office of Institutional Research (*Student Cohort Performance in TASP-Designated College-Level Courses*, 1999) found that in designated college-level courses, ESL students outperformed both native English speakers who had completed developmental courses and students who tested directly into college-level courses.

GOOD PRACTICES FOR ESOL AT THE COMMUNITY COLLEGE

As noted in the research, many colleges meet the challenge of providing appropriate assessment, advisement, instruction, and support services to this growing population of non-native English speakers. The following are some of the good practices exhibited by these institutions:

Faculty Instruction

- Full-time faculty assume leadership roles for curriculum development, program design, and the training and mentoring of adjunct faculty.

- Program coordinators and instructors have backgrounds in TESL.

- Students receive pre- and post-testing so that placement is confirmed and comparative data on student learning is available.

- Each part of the ESL/ESOL program is outcomes-based. Students are given exit competency tests in all skill areas to ensure their preparedness for the next level of coursework.

- ESL/ESOL faculty share equal status with other academic faculty.

- Instruction is delivered as language acquisition rather than remediation. Ideally, the program focuses on English for Academic Purposes (EAP) or specialized language instruction that helps move the students toward their professional or social goal.

- Multiple delivery options are offered to meet the non-native English speakers' varied language needs, continuing education, pre-academic credit, academic credit, learning communities, intensive English programs, vocational ESL

Assessment/Advisement

- A specialized advising center with trained staff provides quality assessment, advising, orienting, mentoring, and tracking for ESL/ESOL students.

- Assessment instruments are designed specifically for non-native English speakers, such as Michigan Test of English Language Proficiency, ACT ESL Placement Test, Michigan English Language Assessment Battery, and Accuplacer Levels of English Proficiency.

- Specially trained advisors provide degree planning, financial aid referral, career advisement, and residency information services.

- Advisors collaborate with ESL/ESOL faculty and staff to coordinate assessment, advising, placement, and instruction.

Administration

- ESL/ESOL is integrated into the strategic planning, budgeting, and organizational structure as an equal partner with all other academic divisions.

- ESL/ESOL is placed within an academic division that focuses on languages rather than remediation.

- Degree credit is granted for ESL/ESOL college-level courses to be counted toward foreign-language or humanities requirements.

- At the early stages of establishing an ESL/ESOL program, some colleges have converted into ESL through a developmental education model in which special sections are taught by special TESL-trained faculty.

Support Services

- TESL-trained tutors provide tutoring services.

- Conversation partners are provided.

- Regular culture education classes are available.

- Involvement in both college and civic communities is encouraged.

- Computer labs with ESL/ESOL software are available.

Research/Evaluation

- Performance data systematically collected and used in ongoing evaluation and follow-up allow for continuous program and curriculum adjustment and improvement.

- The ESL/ESOL program is regularly evaluated through a recognized format such as the TESOL Standards, established by the professional organization Teachers of English to Speakers of Other Languages to provide a self-study format for accrediting ESL programs.

- Student success and retention are tracked and are compared to other populations.

10
WHY BEST PRACTICE IS IMPORTANT

Best practices provide guideposts that are resources for continuous program improvement. They offer a way to share program results and to build on the successes of others. Many of the topics covered in this chapter have been addressed in more detail in other chapters. Those practices that can be classified as best practice are singled out in the context of this chapter.

The quality of developmental education programs varies widely, and its efficacy is frequently questioned. In Texas, for example, despite developmental courses implemented to help students succeed, the number of students passing the state-mandated assessment test, TASP, was declining. The Texas legislature considered eliminating TASP as well as developmental education and engaged a consulting team headed by Hunter Boylan to review the entrance examination (Boylan, et al., 1992) and the effectiveness of developmental education (Boylan & Saxon, 1998). The team found the examination to be valid and reliable. They identified the problem as the disparity in the quality of developmental programs.

Rather than eliminating developmental education, the team recommended aggressive action to strengthen weak programs. The Texas Legislature responded forcefully to the team's findings. They mandated the evaluation and certification of the quality and effectiveness of all developmental programs. While the proposed legislation did not pass, it echoed similar concerns about quality expressed in many state legislatures.

Educators have not done a good job in responding to the concerns of public decision makers. The data about the outcomes of developmental education is very limited, and little is routinely collected. This lack of concrete information is politically damaging. It is clear that program effectiveness must be documented and ineffective programs discontinued.

Legislatures and the public will not continue to support programs unless productivity can be documented.

Nor should we in the field tolerate anything but our best. Raising the competencies and aspirations of underprepared students is essential to preserving our democracy and maintaining a vibrant economy. We should be actively researching best practices, experimenting with those models, and collecting data on students' performance.

> *Raising the competencies and aspirations of underprepared students is essential to preserving our democracy and maintaining a vibrant economy.*

We do know what works in developmental education. This chapter shares some of what has been learned about the components of quality programs and identifies resources for implementing those components.

Elements of Strong Programs

How do we know when a program is effective? What criteria can be used in evaluations? Accreditors and researchers are clear: The key is evidence of student learning, not simply participation. At-risk students who participate in developmental programs must meet their academic or career goals. We know what the results should be. How do we achieve them?

Information in developmental and higher education research provides a blueprint to success. Roueche and Roeuche (1994), McCabe and Day (1998), and Neuburger (1999) offer extensive reviews of the best practices in developmental education. The Exxon Corporation study conducted by Boylan, Bonham, Claxton, and Bliss (1992) and Boylan and Saxon's Texas study (1998) provide comprehensive and compelling information on effective developmental education programs and practices.

Criteria for evaluating program effectiveness should be tied to student-centered goals. In evaluating program effectiveness, it is important to tie data to individual student goals. It is also important to distinguish between students who make appropriate use of the services and those who do not. Prince George's Community College in Maryland has collected data that demonstrates that when students complete the developmental programs, they are successful. Students who do not complete the programs or attend erratically do not have the same success.

Developmental Programs Should Be Comprehensive

Researchers consistently conclude that students should be viewed holistically, with both cognitive and affective needs addressed. Retention and academic success are functions of personal and environmental issues as well as of academic skills (Keimig, 1983; Anderson, 1985; Van, 1994; O'Banion, 1997; Boylan, Bliss, & Bonham, 1997; Boylan & Saxon, 1998; Maxwell, 1997; Neuburger, 1999).

The personal needs of many high-risk students require the most attention. Establishing a program to address these needs is vital to success with developmental students. The principles of adult learning must be incorporated in the pedagogy, and the curriculum must be integrated and in harmony with other campus offerings. Faculty from all disciplines must be part of an active communication network (Boylan, Bonham, & Rodriguez, 2000).

In 1983, calling for greater comprehensiveness and institutionalization of developmental education, Keimig (1983) divided academic interventions into four quality levels:

- Level I–remedial courses (skills-based only)
- Level II–assistance for individual students (e.g., academic tutoring, advising)
- Level III–course-related learning services (labs, CAI, Supplemental Instruction, study groups)
- Level IV–comprehensive learning systems (combination of all levels)

While community colleges tend to emphasize remedial proficiency in math, reading, and writing, the best programs are comprehensive.

The Community College of Denver's Academic Support Center, for example, provides an assortment of services available to all students. The curriculum includes not only skills proficiency, but also learning strategies, academic goal setting, and campus and community acclimatization. Prince

George's Community College (MD) has a strong proficiency program for math, reading, and composition. The college reports, however, that developmental students appear to be more successful when support programs addressing personal and learning strategies supplement the academic program. The Tech Prep programs offered in many Massachusetts community colleges are equally comprehensive. By including curriculum alignment, optional early assessment, course articulation, counseling, and advising, they effectively transition students from high school to college (Brickman & Stockford, 2000).

The Best Developmental Programs are Centralized or Coordinated

Students are best served when all elements of support are combined in a coordinated constellation of services. All support programs should have the shared mission of student success regardless of the different ways they deliver services. The quality of program design and staff credentialing should be commensurate throughout the various support services.

Regular communication of program mission, goals, and objectives is essential. Constituencies both inside and outside developmental programs, including the faculty of college-level courses, must engage in routine dialogue. This communication supports consistency and alignment in content preparation. It is also beneficial for faculty to have taught regular and developmental courses, to better understand the issues related to both experiences (Boylan & Saxon, 1998; Keimig, 1983). Both the College Success Skills Department at Portland Community College and the Academic Support Services Department at Sandhills Community College exemplify this integrated approach.

Students are best served when all elements of support are combined in a coordinated constellation of services.

The College Success Skills Department in Portland has a faculty chair to foster links throughout the campus that are intended to ease student transitions. Academic and developmental faculty members share information and pedagogies with each other. Many faculty members teach in both departments. Campus tutoring programs collaborate and share referral forms and brochures (McCabe & Day, 1998). In a similar way, Sandhill's comprehensive Academic Support Services Department has an advisory committee which includes the chairs of the math and English departments, testing coordinator, dean of instruction, and student development representative. The interaction of this group contributes informed and coordinated decisions.

Ideally, there should be a single administrator responsible for all services for underprepared students. If that is not possible, the directors of the various services should meet regularly to communicate and to coordinate their areas.

Quality Programs Support Qualified Professional Staff

Many developmental educators enter the field with little or no specific training. This lack of background, however, is no excuse to remain uninformed. Adjunct faculty teaching in remedial math, reading, or composition courses should be familiar with the best pedagogies and theories. The college must take responsibility for the professional developmental of this staff (Neuburger, 1999; Boylan & Saxon, 1998; Roeuche & Roeuche, 1994; Van, 1994).

The NADE Self-Evaluation Guide section titled "Program Factors Influencing the Teaching Learning Process" (1995, p. 2) provides a quick guide to quality pedagogical frameworks. Developmental educators are expected to be as familiar with instructional process and the special needs of developmental students as they are with course content. The Supplemental Instruction Center at the University of Missouri, Kansas City (www.umkc.edu/cad/si) provides regular national and regional training opportunities for SI leaders and directors. Colleges that have effective developmental programs assure that both part-time and full-time faculty are well prepared and that their competencies remain current.

Sandhills Community College has a very high ratio of full-time to part-time developmental faculty. They select instructors who have chosen to teach developmental students, and they actively support professional growth of all faculty. This commitment to mission translates into a superior program. Santa Fe Community College hires its adjunct faculty through a screening interview that assures an aptitude for working with developmental students. Part-time faculty are given extensive training and are provided teaching and curriculum supervision by full-time staff. The Developmental Education Services Department of Bucks County College supports its part-time faculty with professional opportunities both on and off campus. Mentoring programs offer guidance and professional growth.

The National Tutor Association has initiated a professional certification program designed to encourage and recognize excellence in professional tutoring, paraprofessional tutoring, and tutor trainer and administrator preparation and development. Colleges have the opportunity to help developmental educators by taking advantage of the many institutes, graduate programs, and conferences that lead to NTA certification.

At the Core: Mandatory Assessment and Placement

Placing students appropriately as a result of assessments is fundamental to student success. Random placement without considering needs, competencies, and learning style is a formula for failure (Roeuche & Roeuche, 1993; Van, 1994; Boylan, Bliss, & Bonham, 1997; Maxwell, 1997; Neuburger, 1999; McCabe, 2000). An effective assessment and placement program, however, requires flexibility and an institutional commitment in both policy and budget. Santa Fe Community College (FL), for example, allows students to be reassessed the first day of class to confirm the appropriateness of their initial placement. If initial placement is inappropriate, students are then correctly placed.

Best Practice Requires Consistent Program Evaluation

A critical best-practice element is systematic program evaluation with data used for program improvement. Traditionally this has been an area of weakness in developmental programs (Levitz & Noel, 1985; Maxwell, 1991; Boylan, Bonham, & Bliss, 1994; Claxton, 1992; Roeuche & Roeuche, 1994; Van, 1994; Casazza & Silverman, 1996; Boylan, Bonham, & Bliss, 1997; Boylan & Saxon, 1998; Neuburger, 1999). McCabe and Day assert:

> Although fewer than 20 percent of the programs surveyed conducted regular, systematic program evaluations, students in evaluated programs are more likely to be successful than those in programs without evaluation programs. (1998, p. 21)

Evaluation is a process, not an activity or event. Both formative and summative evaluations are useful for designing an effective developmental program. Assessment is not a one-time activity; rather, it is evolutionary, ongoing, and incremental. Assessment efforts should be continuous, comprehensive, systematic, integrative, and organic. Regardless of their scope, these efforts should be both qualitative and quantitative (New England Association of Schools and Colleges, 1992, p. 2).

Qualitative information determines the success of affective goals, such as satisfaction with services or improved student self-esteem. Quantitative information measures outcomes data such as learning and retention. Casazza and Silverman (1996) provide an excellent comparison of the differences and value of the methodologies. Maxwell (1996) offers a detailed discussion of how the methods apply to developmental education.

The goal of evaluation, whether formative or summative, qualitative or quantitative, is to provide critical information to aid in making program improvements. Data can be used for promoting a program's strengths or making arguments for appropriate support. But the evaluation process is only best practice when it is integrated into program operations. Information in charts, graphs, and grids, for example, should not be viewed as a static, end event. It is actively used to learn: What story does the data tell? What questions still need to be asked? What further information would be helpful? What is working and what isn't? What action should be taken?

In the formative mode, program decision makers read professional journals, review research, administer surveys, talk to colleagues, conduct self-studies, and consult experts or published standards guides to garner the best ideas and methods. Self-evaluation requires the program director to be diligent in looking for patterns; to be honest, motivated by the desire to improve rather than to protect; to invite different points of view; and to generate thinking, decision making, and action plans.

Summative evaluation requires clearly stated student-centered goals, whether they be graduation, college transfer, or job proficiency. It requires identification of measures to determine whether goals have been met, collection of evaluation data, and a process for making decisions based on the results. Decision makers must be very clear about student-centered goals and continually review the extent to which those goals are being met. If a program follows every principle of best practice but cannot show that student goals are being achieved, then the program fails. Summative results need to be measurable. The integrated evaluation process requires consistent review of how well goals and objectives are being met.

The effectiveness of developmental programs is determined by student outcomes from these programs. Developmental or learning-assistance program directors and data analysts cannot collect appropriate data if the institution does not provide support for this initiative. "An institution's efforts and ability to assess its effectiveness and use the obtained information for its improvement are important indicators of institutional quality" (NEASC *Policy Statement on Institution Effectiveness*, January 22, 1992).

Lopez (1996) points out that, to the detriment of their students, institutions that have poorly organized data collection place little value on assessing student achievement and have no process for linking outcomes information to program improvement Banta (1996) notes:

> Assessment is most effective when undertaken in an environment that is receptive, supportive, and enabling. More specifically, successful assessment requires an environment characterized by effective leadership, administrative commitment, adequate resources (for example, clerical support and money), faculty and staff development opportunities, and time. (p. 62)

Excellent Programs Have Strong Institutional Support

Developmental programs reach excellence when they are nurtured in an institutional culture grounded in belief in the value of all human beings (Boylan & Saxon, 1998; Roeuche & Roeuche, 1993; Van, 1994; Maxwell, 1997; Neuburger, 1999). Developmental and remedial programs should be fully integrated into the life of the institution (Boylan & Saxon, 1998; Neuburger, 1999; McCabe & Day, 1998; Keimig, 1983). Retention is a collaborative and shared concern (Keimig, 1983; Tinto, 1987). The president and board set the standard. Their leadership reinforces the importance of developmental education and helps develop a supportive institutional climate. It creates adequate budgets, services, and staff development.

Prince George's Community College credits the strong commitment of their vice presidents for instruction, continuing education/evening programs, and student services for the close collaboration established between developmental and college-level courses. This support helps students smoothly progress toward their learning goals. The president and board of trustees are equally as dedicated to developmental education and providing budget support. Between 1996 and 1998, Prince George's began 22 new program enhancements (McCabe & Day, 1998).

Sandhills Community College's (NC) administration demonstrates commitment by investing substantially in its developmental education program. In 1995, the institution consolidated all remedial services into an academic support center, funded mandatory assessment and placement, promoted campus collaboration, and provided training and professional staff development.

Developmental faculty and program leaders should be included in program decision making, serve on college committees, and be part of the academic life of the campus. The budget should be sufficient to employ high-quality staff and support them with appropriate professional development. Pay and benefits for developmental faculty should be commensurate with campus standards.

Best-Practice Tools

In addition to the literature on best practice and program design, developmental education directors can use expert consultants or be guided by standards published in the field. Instruments such as CAS Standards for Learning Assistance Programs, NADE guides, and CRLA Tutor Training Certification are paths to successful programs. They provide an opportunity for directors to compare their program components with best-practice components. These outside sources particularly help directors whose summative evaluations show that students are not meeting program goals.

The Council on Advancement of Standards in Higher Education (CAS) has been promulgating standards since the early 1980s. Periodically, the Council updates its *Book of Professional Standards in Higher Education* (Miller, 1999) and offer directors important guidelines. CAS standards are based on a belief that all quality programs actively address the following components:

mission, program, leadership, organization and management, human resources, financial resources, facilities and equipment, legal responsibilities, equal opportunity, access and affirmative action, campus and community relations, diversity, ethics, and assessment and evaluation.

The *NADE Self-Evaluation Guides: Models for Assessing Learning Assistance/Developmental Educational Programs* (Clark-Thayer, 1995) apply the CAS self-evaluation model to specific developmental programs such as tutoring services, developmental coursework, adjunct instruction, and program factors that influence the teaching and learning process. Both *CAS Standards for Learning Assistance Programs* and *NADE Self-Evaluation Guides* are tools program directors use to assure best practice in program design. These instruments stimulate staff to engage in thought-provoking dialogue and comprehensively review their programs.

The Tutor Training Certification offered by the College Reading and Learning Association (CRLA) (Gier, 1994) is an outstanding tool for guiding tutor training programs. Use of CRLA Tutor Certification encourages quality programs (Boylan, Bonham, Bliss, & Claxton, 1992).

NADE Program Certification

Programs seriously striving for best practice will work toward NADE Program Certification. This certification, launched in 1999 to "recognize programs that meet or exceed criteria of good practices as defined by professional research and literature of the field" (NADE Certification Review Manual, p. 2), embodies both formative and summative evaluation in a dynamic, integrated process. The *NADE Self-Evaluation Guides* are employed in a self-study. They compare program components to best practice in tutoring services, developmental coursework programs, and adjunct instructional programs including course-based support such as Supplemental Instruction. Designed to be flexible, the *Guides* offer commonalities while still allowing freedom to embrace the varied context in which specific programs exist.

To apply for certification, programs must have written mission, goals, and objectives statements for the developmental education program. For the component being certified, tutoring services, developmental coursework, or adjunct instructional programs, there must be an articulated theory base or model used as reference for decisions made in program design and pedagogy; an evaluation process that is systematically used to determine if student-centered goals have been met; evaluation results that are used to make decisions about program improvements; three years of recent evaluation data showing positive student outcomes and trend data in decision-making; and CRLA tutor training certification in process or completed.

Applicants are required to attend an all-day training institute covering formative self-evaluation, summative evaluation, program decision-making, and the certification process. Certification Board members are available via e-mail for questions throughout the application process. NADE returns unsuccessful applications with guidance on areas that require strengthening in order to achieve certification. Three levels of summative evaluation are used. **Primary Certification** describes how many, how much, or how often something was done; **Secondary Certification** refers to short-term effects such as gain in test scores, completion rates, and course grades. **Tertiary Certification** examines long-term effects such as retention from year to year and GPA upon graduation (Boylan, 1996).

General Certification acknowledges that a program regularly collects utilization and profile data that are reviewed for patterns, program improvement, and other bases of decision-making. Programs certified at this level have not shown data to prove successful student outcomes. General certification data for a developmental math course whose goal is to prepare students for college math include the number of students who finish the course, student demographics, student attendance patterns, student satisfaction surveys, and average number of developmental courses taken before students move to college courses.

NADE defines Advanced and Distinguished Certification a little more narrowly than the Boylan model. **Advanced Certification** describes a program that has demonstrated excellence in fulfilling the general category and shows both quantitatively and qualitatively that all of the student-centered goals are being met. Secondary data for a developmental math course might include higher post-test scores after remediation, C or better

GPA in the follow-up college math courses, higher pass rates of the math section of college entrance/placement tests, and retention from semester to semester.

NADE reserves its highest category, **Distinguished Certification**, for those programs that show excellence at the general and advanced level and follow their students through to final goals. Examples of these data from a 1999 report by the State Board of Community Colleges in North Carolina are performance of college transfer students, employer satisfaction with graduates, employment status of graduates, and client satisfaction with customized training. This recognition requires a comprehensive program whose goals extend beyond course remediation to long-term student achievement. Certified programs will have at least a three-year pattern of data collection and decision-making. Certification is for seven years, after which programs can apply for recertification.

Making Change

Many developmental educators recognize their institution's shortcomings in providing a quality environment. They return from conferences or read about exciting new ideas to improve student success and then despair over their inability to make changes. After a decade of using institutional effectiveness data, Hudgins and Williams (1997, p. 64) offered specific statements regarding technique for reforming both actions and attitude toward bringing about program improvement:

- Institutional effectiveness is a journey, not a destination.

- Trustee support and involvement are important.

- Executive leadership is essential.

- Faculty participation is integral to the enhancement of teaching and learning.
- Data must be used for improvement, not punishment.

- Patience is essential.

- Flexibility and change are critical to the success of the process.

We know that improvements are needed in most colleges; change, however, does not happen overnight. People need time to adapt to change. Commitment and ownership must be developed. Successful change agents break a three- to five-year plan into increments to be implemented sequentially, often starting small, with a pilot. A pilot effort is a trial that can fail, be modified, and begin anew. Early achievement sets a foundation for the next steps. Patience is imperative; the stage must be prepared for each step forward.

Some battles can never be won, so time and energy should not be wasted on them. Some battles can be won at a later time. Have all persuasive information handy at all times to be able to reference it at opportune moments. Most important, never lose sight of the goal. Many times, change can be made if the person driving the change is flexible about how the goal is reached. Try to effect a compromise that will achieve the shared goal.

Julius, in his *Memo from Machiavelli* (Julius, 1999), suggests that change makers should "advance the notion of 'mutual interests' rather than focusing on the positions of those who disagree." Start with the goal on which everyone can agree and then work together through participation and patience. "Interpersonal relations…is constantly building good will and negotiating in good faith, not in fear…." (Covey, 1992, p. 254).

Successfully making change takes patience, perseverance, humanity, and constant communication. It is difficult and challenging but it is possible with the right attitude and thoughtful participatory planning. Institutional environment and culture profoundly influence developmental programs. Committed practitioners can realize program improvement, especially when backed by strong institutional support and by accrediting agencies aggressively promoting institutional effectiveness.

RESOURCES

Center for Supplemental Instruction
(www.umkc.edu/cad/si)

Council on Advancement of Standards in Higher Education (CAS)
(www.cas.edu)
- *Blue Book on Standards in Higher Education* (includes Learning Assistance Programs)

College Reading and Learning Association (CRLA)
(www.crla.net\Welcome.htm)
- *Journal of College Reading and Learning*
- Program Certification for Tutor Training Programs
- Annual conference
- Occasional special symposia

National Association of Developmental Education (NADE)
(www.nade.net)
- Extensive web links to learning assistance/developmental education resources
- NADE Program Certification for Tutoring Services, Developmental Coursework and Adjunct Instructional Programs (course-based support such as supplemental instruction)
- NADE Self-Evaluation Guides: models for program effectiveness
- Annual conference
- Local and regional chapters with conferences

National Center for Developmental Education (NCDE)
(www.ncde.appstate.edu)
- *Journal of Developmental Education*
- Research in Developmental Education (RIDE)
- Kellogg Institute
- Periodic research conferences

National College Learning Center Association (NCLCA)

(www.eiu.edu/~lrnasst/nclca/index.html)
- *Learning Assistance Review*
- Annual conference

National Tutoring Association (NTA)

(www.ntatutor.org)
- Certification for professional tutors, paraprofessional tutors and tutor trainers and administrators
- Annual conferences

New York College Learning Skills Association (NYCLSA)

(www.rit.edu/~jwsldc/nyclsa/index.shtml)
- *Journal of Research and Teaching*
- Annual conference

Winter Institute for Learning Assistance Professionals

(www.pvc.maricipa.edu/~/sche)

11
EFFECTIVE PROGRAMS AND PRACTICES

Τhe common threads that run through all of the best programs and practices are institutional support, coordinated services, emphasis on personal development and, of greatest importance, committed staff. Most community colleges simply do not do the best that they can for their underprepared students. There are, however, many examples of effective programs and practices. Experience is the best teacher, and even colleges with outstanding programs can learn from the experiences and successes of others. The following brief descriptions of effective programs and practices are provided as a resource.

Effective Programs

1. Central Carolina Community College

Contact: Nancy Turner, Dean
College Address: 1105 Kelly Dr., Sanford, NC 27330
Telephone Number: (919) 718-7222
E-Mail Address: nturner@gw.ccarolina.cc.nc.us

Structure

The Central Carolina Community College Developmental Studies program is centralized. The organizational structure includes a program dean, department chair, two developmental coordinators for two satellite campuses, three English faculty, three reading faculty, five math faculty, and a varying number of part-time instructors.

All of the developmental courses are five contact hours, four semester credit hours, or both. The CCCC program is self-paced and mastery-based, with a required competency level of 80 percent. All courses are taught in a combination of computer-laboratory and traditional classroom environments. To guide the students through the course, and to provide additional practice, the departmental faculty have prepared an in-house ancillary to accompany the textbooks or software.

Components

A variety of teaching materials is available as students work to meet the 80 percent competency level in each of their developmental courses. All courses have computer software relevant to the specific subject area. In math and algebra, videotapes are also available to explain each section in the textbooks. When students purchase their math textbooks, they also purchase a Personal Identification Number (PIN) to allow them to access the software on the Internet, to give them the option of free tutor services provided by the publisher, and to provide a study guide. In algebra, students purchase a textbook, software, and digital CD-ROM with video clips to further explain the problems being discussed. In English, students purchase the textbook and a practice CD-ROM.

CCCC has mandatory placement. All students are tested using the Computerized Placement Test (CPT). Students who initially score within 10 points of the requirement for the English or mathematics course in their chosen curriculum qualify for a retest. However, if the required score is not met, the student must sign up for the appropriate developmental course. The offerings include one level of basic mathematics, one level of reading, one level of math, and two levels of algebra. At the end of the semester, all students are given the CPT as the final exam.

Using raw scores, the following are the requirements and the course that must be entered or repeated if the required score is not met:

Course	Required Score
Eng 090	Sentence Skills < 86
Math 060	Arithmetic < 57
Math 070	Arithmetic ≥ 57 and Algebra < 38
Math 080	Arithmetic ≥ 57 and Algebra $38 < x < 70$
Red 090	Reading Comprehension < 80

CCCC's support system includes a special-populations director who informs the faculty of a student's special needs. Also, developmental students are advised to take a reduced load (maximum of four courses) during the term of developmental course enrollment. This approach is used to avoid overloading or discouraging at-risk students while encouraging completion of developmental courses as soon as possible. A dual advising system provides the student with a developmental advisor and a curriculum-specific advisor, who work together to develop a successful plan.

One of the distinctive features of the CCCC Developmental Program is the distance education option. Students may take Basic Math, Elementary Algebra, Intermediate Algebra, and Sentence Skills via distance education. The mathematics courses are taught using cassettes and other blended media; the developmental English course is offered online.

Outcomes

Initially, concern was expressed about the success of developmental students taking distance learning options. The college has been pleased with the results: Basic Math, 89 percent pass rate; Elementary Algebra, 90 percent pass rate; Intermediate Algebra, 100 percent pass rate; Sentence Skills, 75 percent pass rate. Pass Rate is defined as the percentage of students who made the required score on the standardized exit exam (CPT).

Another feature of the CCCC program is the set of guidelines designated by the North Carolina Community College System. These guidelines are known as the Twelve Performance Measures, an accountability plan for each of the 59 community colleges in North Carolina. Demonstrating the importance of developmental studies at the community college level, the state has designated two of the 12 to deal with developmental studies.

The first measure is that all developmental courses must have a 70 percent pass rate. The second measure is that there should be no statistically significant difference in the success of developmental students and college-level students in their first required curriculum course in English, mathematics, and social science. The first year of data was reported to NCCCS in the spring of 2001, for the 1999-2000 academic year. For the pass rate performance measure, math and algebra have an average pass rate of from 74 percent to 100 percent. A redesign of the Developmental English course is in the works that will implement an additional level of reading to help meet this measure.

Results of the second performance measure–that developmental students make a C or higher in their first curriculum course compared to their college-level peers–was met with the results illustrated in Figure 11.1.

FIGURE 11.1 SUCCESS RATES OF DEVELOPMENTAL AND COLLEGE-LEVEL STUDENTS

	Percent of developmental students making a C or better	Percent of college-level students making a C or better
English	92 %	90 %
Reading	91 %	88 %
Math	100 %	90 %

The CCCC developmental program enjoys overall success primarily because of the dedication of the faculty and the teamwork approach to the program. The faculty are committed to using a variety of teaching techniques and resources. The use of technology in the lab and collaborative learning format in the classroom add to the success of the program. The developmental studies faculty members are held more accountable than the majority of other faculty on campus because the students must make the required score on the standardized exit exam (CPT) in order to pass the course. This requirement has stimulated the students to perform even beyond their own expectations sometimes, and compelled faculty to motivate these students through their developmental program.

2. COMMUNITY COLLEGE OF DENVER

Contact: Levi Crespin, Dean
College Address: CB 600, P.O. Box 173363, Denver, CO 80217
Telephone Number: (303) 556-2481
E-Mail Address: Levi.Crespin@ccd.cccoes.edu

Structure

The Center for Educational Advancement at the Community College of Denver is made up of a number of programs that provide developmental education services. These services include the Academic Support Center; Student Support Services; Special Learning Support; Reading/Study Skills; Math, Writing, and English as a Second Language (ESL) support labs; English as a Second Language, the General Equivalency Diploma program, and the Testing Center. A dean oversees the operation of the Center, with each program run by a director. Each discipline area also has a program coordinator.

Upon entry to CCD, students are administered The College Board's Accuplacer Computerized Placement Test in addition to a local study-skills instrument. As of fall 2001, the Colorado Community College state system, following new state-mandated legislation, implemented mandatory placement into basic skills courses. However, CCD has always strongly advised students to enroll in developmental courses before entering college-level classes.

Components

The three levels of development are Reading, English, and ESL courses, and there are four levels of mathematics. Of the students testing for placement into courses for fall 2001, 61 percent placed into developmental English, 71 percent into developmental reading, 61 percent into study skills, and 84 percent into developmental math.

Nine percent of our students are in the ESL program. There are numerous support services for students, including the Academic Support Center, Student Support Services; Special Learning Support; Reading/Study

Skills; Math, Writing, and ESL support labs, and the GED Institute. In addition, there are numerous special initiatives to assist first-generation and low-income students. The North, East, and West campuses provide additional access points for students to enroll in developmental education courses, which include GED and ESL classes. The branch campuses offer open-entry, open-exit classes throughout the year. The Community College of Denver has also invested in the case management approach to help ease first-time students' transition to a supportive educational setting.

The Community College of Denver provides one-third of all remedial education in Colorado public higher education. Developmental education courses account for 44 percent of the total headcount enrollment. Of these developmental education enrollees, 58 percent are women, 59.3 percent are people of color, and 9 percent are ESL students. The cumulative GPA of first-time developmental students who finish one year is 2.94. The subsequent success of developmental students going into English Composition is 71.7 percent, and for College Algebra the success rate is 75.6 percent. FiscalYear 1998 data from a CCD study conducted in October 1999 indicate that 52 percent of first-time students were enrolled in the developmental courses; 26 percent of developmental course enrollees are full-time students; completion rate for developmental courses is 72 percent; and 76 percent of new students require at least one developmental education course.

Relative to other Colorado community colleges, CCD has the largest number and percentages of students in developmental education courses. CCD also has the largest number of multiple developmental coursetakers. And statewide, 37 percent of the people of color enrolled in developmental education are at CCD, including 46 percent of the African-Americans, 37 percent of the Asian/Pacific Islanders, and 35 percent of the Hispanics (CCD Blue Ribbon Panel Response). In fiscal year 1999, CCD reached a milestone when over half of the graduates (50.7 percent) and transfers (55.5 percent) were people of color. In Fiscal Year 1986, 13 percent of the graduates and transfers were people of color. Approximately 35 percent of the adult population in the CCD service area consists of people of color.

Outcomes

In view of an overwhelming 60 percent of our students being first-generation college students, and many of them also being economically challenged, CCD has created a variety of learning options and support services. The college's Academic Support Center (ASC) offers free tutoring in ESL, mathematics, reading, study skills, and writing. The center operates Monday through Saturday, 72 hours per week, and offers one-on-one tutoring, small-group work, and instruction enhanced by faculty and peer tutors and mentors. In 1998-99, the ASC served 41 percent of the college's students with a course-related success rate of 89 percent. In addition to the ASC, the Special Learning Support program assists students with learning disabilities or specific learning needs. Through the federally-funded TRIO program, Student Support Services assists first-generation, disabled, or low-income students.

In 1999, students who completed a developmental education course of study persisted, graduated, and transferred at higher rates than the college's average student; therefore, developmental education completion has become a predictor of success. Furthermore, cohort tracking reveals no difference in developmental students' success on the basis of age, ethnicity, or gender.

CCD strives to include student learning and student success in all of its decision making. Data from courses and support services are evaluated annually to determine how effectively CCD programs are helping students. This information gives a good picture of where CDC is in relation to college goals. It assists in the next year's planning process and in deciding what improvements need to be made. Through this process, CDC has found several keys to success in developmental education:

- Institutional assessment, planning, and budgeting
- Institutional commitment
- Cultural sensitivity
- Entry-level assessment
- Exit competencies
- Computer technology

- Tutors and mentors
- Professional development priority
- Accountability
- Integration of grant-funded efforts
- Case management
- Integrated advising
- Community outreach

CCD has numerous other programs that help all students be successful, but it recognizes the critical mission of educating the underprepared student. "Our country cannot afford to lose the productivity of these citizens," wrote then-CCD President Byron McClenney in an issue of *The Presidency*, published by the American Council on Education. "The promise of equal opportunity demands that we offer students a second chance" (Fall 1999, p. 23).

Christine Johnson, CCD's new president, has identified "increasing student access and success" as her top goal. She says, "Stewardship of CCD's mission and strengthening the organizational culture to support learning must remain at the core of CCD's beliefs."

3. KIRKWOOD COMMUNITY COLLEGE

Contact: Chuck Hinz, Dean, Learning Services
College Address: 6301 Kirkwood Blvd. SW, Cedar Rapids, IA 52404
Telephone Number: (319) 398-5574
E-Mail Address: chinz@kirkwood.cc.ia.us

Structure

Learning Services is one of the nine instructional departments located within the instruction branch of the college. Those departments include Arts and Science (math and science, English, humanities, and social science), Applied Science and Technology (agricultural sciences, industrial technologies, health sciences, and business and information technologies), and Learning Services. A dean administers each department and reports to the vice president of instruction. The vice president reports directly to the president of the college. This organizational structure places Learning Services at the same level of services and access to central administration as all other instructional departments. The Learning Services department employs approximately 32 full- and part-time faculty and support positions.

Components and Outcomes

Learning Services provides an umbrella of student support services that covers developmental education services as well as assessment, preparation, instruction (both preparatory and supplemental), student support services, tutoring services, the test center, assistive technologies, workplace communication, and disability services for both students and staff.

The department is responsible for assessing all incoming students' academic skills. This is accomplished by administering the COMPASS placement test. Students whose placement test results indicate the need for developmental coursework in reading, writing, or math are referred to department faculty by the advising center. The college does not mandate enrollment in developmental courses; however, many students choose to enroll in developmental courses, either to prepare themselves academically for higher-level courses or to obtain supplemental instruction while enrolled in higher-level courses.

Department courses include College Prep (a 12-credit learning community designed to prepare students both academically and culturally for college success), College Reading, Basic Writing, Study Skills, Basic Math, Pre-Algebra, Academic Prep for Health, and Academic Prep for Culinary Arts. In addition, students can register for credit-bearing Supplemental Instruction for writing and math courses. These courses (PA Writing and PA Math) provide Supplemental Instruction for students enrolled in writing courses taught by the English department and math courses taught by the Math/Science department. During the 2000 calendar year, over 1,325 students were enrolled in these developmental courses, and of those students, 82 percent were retained to completion of the courses.

In addition to these developmental courses, the department also offers several math courses specifically designed for numerous Applied Science and Technology majors. The department offers the Workplace Communication Skills curriculum, which consists of three courses Workplace Communication Skills, Advanced Workplace Communication Skills, and Oral Communications in the Workplace. These courses emphasize applied writing and applied oral communication and are included in many of the Applied Science and Technology programs. During the calendar year 2000, 669 students enrolled in the Workplace Communication curriculum, representing 32 different Applied Science and Technology majors. The retention rate for these courses was 92 percent. For the written communication skills courses, the average pre-test for students was 47 percent and the average post-test was 78.6 percent.

The Learning Services department also administers the collegewide tutoring program. Any student enrolled in a credit course can receive two hours of free tutoring per week for up to two courses. Both individual and group tutoring are provided. For the 2000 calendar year, over 825 students received tutoring services.

The Learning Services department also administers the TRIO-funded Student Support Services Program, which provides retention and support services to first-generation, economically disadvantaged, or disabled college students. Counseling and writing support services are provided to students to help them complete their educational program, graduate, and transfer to other institutions. Learning Services also oversees the Perkins Vocational Education Service, which provides individual assessment and follow-along services to eligible Perkins students enrolled in any of the Applied Science and Technology Programs.

Assistive Technology services are any of the services that directly assist an individual with a disability in the selection, acquisition, or use of an assistive technology device. Some examples of assistive technology available to students through the Learning Services department include screen-reader software, voice-recognition software, word-prediction software, polarized screen for monitor, closed-circuit TV device, magnification, work lamps, transcription machines, ergonomic keyboards, large monitors, computer accessibility, TDD/TTY, and sign-language interpreters.

The Learning Services department implements and oversees disability accommodation services for students and staff. Any student requesting accommodation services based on a disability is assigned a case manager who works directly with that student to assess needs and determine accommodations, and with the student and faculty members to implement the accommodation plan. During the calendar year 2000, 527 students received accommodation services through the case management system. The system of academic accommodation includes alternative test taking, assistive technology, and a very extensive books-on-tape program with over 600 books and documents on audiotape.

The Learning Services department cooperates with the local K-12 Area Education Agency to provide a transition program for students who were enrolled in special education while in high school. This program, known as VITAL (Vocational Individualized Training and Learning) provides a college-level resource-room service to transition students enrolled in Applied Science and Technology majors. The resource room is staffed by certified special education teachers who provide an array of educational support and developmental services to students enrolled in the Applied Science and Technology programs. The VITAL program enrolls approximately 85 students each year and has a retention rate of 86 percent.

Factors Contributing to Success

The effectiveness of the program can be attributed to several factors, beginning with the administrative structure. Because the Learning Services department is placed at the same administrative level as the other academic departments within the instructional branch, the services offered by the department are viewed as valuable and integral to the health of the institution. This provides the basis for a very strong culture within the college that developmental services and academic support services for students are given facts of life.

A second factor for the success of the program is the dedication and energy level of the staff. They exhibit a high degree of professionalism and view their responsibilities as having utmost importance.

A third factor in program effectiveness is the involvement of the staff within all aspects of the college environment. Many members of the department serve on collegewide committees and teach other courses within their disciplines but outside of the Learning Services department. The staff maintains proactive and high profile within the institution, contributing to a general culture of student success within the entire college.

4. Oakton Community College

Contact: Trudy Bers, Senior Director, Research, Curriculum and Planning
College Address: 1600 E. Golf Rd., Des Plaines, IL 60016
Telephone Number: (847) 635-1894
E-Mail Address: tbers@oakton.edu

Structure

Oakton Community College serves the North Shore suburbs of Chicago, with a well-educated, affluent, and ethnically diverse population and a wide-ranging economy characterized by a large number of small employers in professional, retail, financial, service, and small manufacturing industries. Schools are well financed and of exceptional quality. Parents and educators focus on moving secondary students to college; many high schools report over 90 percent of graduates go on to postsecondary education, most at four-year colleges and universities.

More than three dozen colleges and universities are located in Oakton or within an easy commute of the district. Students regularly move among these institutions, and few Oakton students enroll directly from high school, remain to earn an associate degree, and then transfer. In fact, more students from local high schools attend other schools first and then return to Oakton than attend Oakton as their first college after high school. In addition, Oakton draws thousands of summer school students who attend other colleges and universities during the regular academic year.

These points are important, because for many Oakton students the college is perceived and used as an "occasional" institution where they can remediate academic deficiencies, earn a few college credits before transferring, take courses to learn new job-related skills, prepare for a new career, or learn for personal enrichment. About 20 percent of Oakton students already have a bachelor's degree or higher.

Oakton's remedial education programs and services are structured through both academic departments and the college's academic support unit, Instructional Support Services (ISS). Remedial English and mathematics courses are developed, scheduled, and taught through the English and mathematics departments, respectively. Both full-time and part-time faculty teach courses. All full-time and many part-time faculty are qualified to teach college-level as well as remedial courses in their disciplines.

Placement testing, tutoring, academic support workshops, and other academic assistance programs are offered through ISS, housed within Oakton's Academic Affairs area (as are the English and mathematics departments). ISS staff work closely with academic faculty to ensure that support services align with academic offerings.

Tutoring and other academic support programs are offered free of charge to students. Peer, professional, and faculty tutors provide assistance to students. Tutors participate in a required training program and are regularly evaluated by ISS supervisors.

Components

Placement. Oakton uses the Degrees of Reading Power for reading course placement, a locally developed writing test (WSAT) for composition course placement, and the COMPASS for mathematics placement. The WSAT is a written essay graded holistically by a cadre made up of primarily faculty readers trained to place students at one of six levels of composition courses ranging from very basic remediation to honors level. Two readers evaluate all student work; if there is a discrepancy in scores, a third reader evaluates the work. Writing placement tests from students who identify themselves as non-native speakers of English, or whose writing so suggests, are scored by specially trained English as a Second Language (ESL) evaluators.

Students who wish to take English composition and selected other courses are required to take the English placement tests. Students who wish to take mathematics are required to take the mathematics placement test. In addition, all students seeking to register for their twelfth credit or beyond at the college must take placement tests, even if they do not intend to take English or mathematics. Students who present evidence of having successfully completed 24 or more credits of college-level work elsewhere may have placement tests waived unless they plan to register for English or mathematics courses. Students who provide evidence of successful completion of mathematics courses at a level higher than their placement test results may appeal their placement to a member of the mathematics faculty who has the authority to override COMPASS placements.

The college has a large number of ESL students, estimated to comprise some 20 percent of the student population. Most are immigrants; only a few are in the United States on F-1 student visas. They speak more than 50 different languages, and while many have obtained at least part of their K-12 education in the United States, they have English language deficiencies, particularly in writing.

English and mathematics faculty members determine placement test cut-off scores. Students are not permitted to register for courses higher than the level into which they test, except in the case of the mathematics appeal.

Courses. Oakton offers a total of 12 ESL courses, all at the remedial level (four reading courses, five in writing, and three in speaking or listening). The college also offers special sections of English 101: Composition I for non-native speakers. In regular remedial English, Oakton offers a total of nine courses (three in reading, four in writing, and two in vocabulary or study skills). There are seven remedial mathematics courses, with Elementary Algebra the course most frequently taken. Intermediate Algebra is counted for college credit toward a degree, but does not satisfy general education requirements and is not always accepted by four-year schools, many of which count this course at the remedial level.

Outcomes

Placement. Annually, about 3,000 students take placement tests, though not all take tests in both English and mathematics. Of students taking English tests, about 40 percent place into developmental reading (15 percent into ESL reading), and 50 percent place into developmental writing (20 percent into ESL writing). Of students taking mathematics tests, about two-thirds place into remedial mathematics and another 10 to 15 percent place into Intermediate Algebra.

Academic Achievement. Data indicate that 27 percent of students whose first writing course was an ESL course eventually passed English 101. Nearly half (45 percent) of students who began in regular remedial writing courses eventually passed English 101. These data document success for remedial courses for students who enroll eventually in English 101. Another way to look at data is to examine passing rates in English 101 of students who initially placed into and took remedial or ESL writing, and who persisted and enrolled in English 101. Eighty-four percent of ESL students and 80 percent of regular remedial students passed English 101. Interestingly, 78 percent of students whose first writing course was English 101 passed the course. Taking these two sets of findings together, we learn that remedial students who persist to English 101 do well once they get there, but many students do not continue into English 101. Some transfer elsewhere, some stay at Oakton but do not enroll in other English courses, and some leave school altogether, having acquired the English language or other skills for which they came in the first place. Some, of course, leave because they are not achieving academically or for a myriad of unrelated reasons, including family or work obligations and finances.

A 1998 Fiscal Year study of mathematics students indicated that students testing directly into Intermediate Algebra were succeeding (earning grades of C or better) at a somewhat higher rate (79 percent) than were students who first tested in remedial-level algebra, completed the course, and then entered Intermediate Algebra (70 percent). An analysis of the 1,511 students who placed into remedial mathematics through the summer of 1997 indicated that only 849 of them subsequently enrolled in college-level mathematics courses. Very few students who placed into the lowest-level mathematics courses eventually enrolled and earned a grade of C or better in college-level mathematics courses.

A major contributor to the success of the Oakton Community College developmental education program is the strong collaboration among faculty and staff responsible for assessment testing and placement, student advisement, course and curriculum development, instruction, and academic support services. Together they provide a rich, learner-centered environment in which students have optimal opportunities for assistance and success.

The collaboration across the college contributes to the program's effectiveness. The following components are fully integrated to help students achieve academic success:

- Placement in developmental courses

- Monitoring of course progress and exit testing in reading and writing

- Centralized support services staffed by professionals who provide tutoring, student success courses, athletes' intervention services, services for students with disabilities, Project Succeed (for underachieving students), and a mentoring-based retention program for students on academic warning or probation

- Computer labs with an array of software for supplemental coursework

- Study-skills workshops and individual consultations with study-skills specialists

- Test-performance analysis services for faculty and students

- ESL and non-native student assistance including academic support and advising

- TRIO federal grant program to offer academic support for first-generation and low-income students

- Office of Institutional Research involvement in special studies to assess student learning outcomes and to use information for course, program, and service improvement

5. Owens Community College

Contact: Gerald Bazer, Dean of the Arts and Sciences Division, Acting
    Chair, Developmental Education Department
College Address: Oregon Rd., P.O. Box 10000, Toledo, OH 43699-1947
Telephone Number: (419) 661-7545
E-Mail Address: gbazer@owens.cc.oh.us

Structure

Developmental education comprises one academic department within the Arts and Sciences division. The department has a chair and assistant chair who report to the dean of the college's Arts and Sciences division. The dean reports to the vice president, Academic Affairs who in turn reports directly to the college's president. At present, 21 full-time faculty members (24 percent of the division's 87 full-time faculty) and a large contingent of adjunct faculty teach within developmental education.

Components

Developmental education courses consist of two levels of reading, three levels of writing, two levels of mathematics, and three General Studies courses: Career and Life Decisions, College Success Steps, and Job Search Skills.

Students are placed into appropriate levels of reading, writing, and mathematics based upon results from COMPASS measures. Students are also administered either a locally developed or a nationally standardized instrument during the first week of classes to ensure appropriate placement.

Student support services include a reading and study skills laboratory, a writing center, a mathematics laboratory, tutorial services, an early alert system, a developmental-education computer laboratory, disability resources, advising, and counseling. Professional mentors staff the first three services throughout the week when classes are scheduled.

Outcomes

A student survey is provided each semester for students enrolled in developmental courses. Students respond to 10 questions through five forced choices ranging from Strongly Agree to Strongly Disagree. Each semester, significant numbers of students across all sections of reading, writing, and mathematics select Strongly Agree or Agree.

The College's Institutional Research Office tracks success in college-level courses of students who complete developmental education courses. Current data indicate that more than 70 percent of students passing developmental English courses are successful in all subsequent college-level coursework in English. Another 14 percent are successful in some of their English coursework. More than 60 percent of students who pass developmental mathematics are successful in all subsequent college-level coursework in math. Another 14 percent are successful in some of their math coursework.

SPECIAL FEATURES

- Classes are small. No more than 15 students per class take reading and writing; no more than 25 at one time take mathematics courses.

- Courses are self-paced in the lower sections of mathematics, with two faculty assigned to each section.

- Opportunity is provided for students to complete both levels of developmental math within one semester.

- Mathematics Anxiety sections are offered in the Basic Algebra course. Telecourse sections are offered in Basic Algebra.

- For students whose writing placement examination indicates borderline between developmental and college-level writing, a course is offered that bridges the two, allowing a student to complete the developmental material and the first college-level writing material within one semester, earning three credits toward the college degree.

- Students are enrolled in a college credit program while taking one or more developmental courses, which avoids any stigma of being labeled a developmental student.

- Integrated sections of writing and reading are team-taught by senior faculty.

- A developmental education computer laboratory, surrounded by regular college classrooms, is offered which allows students to go directly from their classes to the lab to draft, edit, and complete written work, and then return to classes.

- Each developmental education course is competency based, with a faculty-approved set of outcomes

FACTORS CONTRIBUTING TO EFFECTIVENESS

- Faculty, whether professors, instructors, or adjuncts, have assignments totally devoted to developmental education. Senior as well as new faculty teach developmental courses as their entire teaching load.

- There is a serious commitment to employing full-time faculty within the developmental education department.

- A national and Ohio perspective on cutting-edge developmental education practices and philosophy shapes professional development faculty activities. Concurrently during 2001-2002, the presidents of the National Association for Developmental Education (NADE) and the Ohio Association for Developmental Education (OADE) were Owens faculty. OADE's *Journal of Teaching and Learning* is co-edited by Owens faculty. Annually, Owens faculty attend and present at the conventions of OADE, NADE, the College Reading and Learning Association (CRLA), and the American Mathematics Association of Two-Year Colleges (AMATYC). The college provides all professional development funding.

- Regular evaluation takes place to ensure that student outcomes are being realized through collegewide, ongoing outcomes assessment procedures.

- Administrative support reaches all the way to the president's office.

- Advisors, counselors, faculty, and academic administrators enjoy close working relationships.

6. RICHLAND COLLEGE, DALLAS COUNTY COMMUNITY COLLEGE DISTRICT

Contact: Mary K. Darin, Dean
College Address: 12800 Abrams Rd., Dallas, TX 75243
Telephone Number: (972) 238-6231
E-Mail Address: mkdarin@dcccd.edu

Structure

Developmental math, reading, and writing courses are centralized at Richland through the Human and Academic Development Division. ESOL is included with other language instruction in the World Languages, Cultures, and Communications Division. The Human and Academic Development and World Languages Divisions are equal partners with all other academic divisions of the college and report through instructional deans to the college's chief academic officer.

Components

Students are required by state law to be tested in basic skills and to remediate each term until the failed areas of the state exam, TASP, are passed. The student registration system will not allow students who have failed TASP to enroll without registering for a developmental course in at least one of the failed areas. Scores from the following are valid for placement: TASP (Texas Academic Skills Program), MAPS, Accuplacer, COMPASS

Full-time professional developmental educators are responsible for the college's extensive multilevel curriculum in developmental math, reading, and writing and in ESOL. Non degree bearing institutional credits and performance grades are awarded in developmental education classes. Students who fail to attend and participate appropriately in their developmental courses are administratively withdrawn from all college-level courses.

Richland's developmental education programs draw heavily upon the theories of self-regulation and self-efficacy. Many Richland students lack self-regulation and are therefore considered at-risk; the goal is to change this deficit into a benefit by transforming the students into lifelong self-learners. While the practices employed to achieve this goal are eclectic and vary by discipline, developmental math, reading, writing, and ESOL programs are united in their efforts to produce self-learners through a demanding curriculum and a responsive learning environment. These qualities of challenge and responsiveness pervade Richland's developmental program. The exigency of our developmental math, reading, and writing programs emanates chiefly from the fact that the courses are integrated into the degree-credit curriculum. While a demanding developmental studies program might challenge the students, the supportive environment in which they learn ensures they need not face these challenges alone. Small class sizes, extraordinary cultural and racial diversity, a variety of learning modalities, and an integrated tutoring and learning center are just a few of the assets that make Richland College's developmental education programs exceptional learning communities. Students benefit greatly from the small class sizes: math sections are limited to 25 students, reading and writing sections are capped at 18, and ESOL sections are limited to 15.

Outcomes

Both formative and summative evaluation processes are employed. Richland uses internal and external benchmarking techniques to extensively review our developmental programs and services. A yearlong national study to identify best practices in developmental education was conducted by the American Productivity & Quality Center and the Continuous Quality Improvement Network. Richland was selected in this blind study as one of five best-practice institutions in developmental education. In addition, the Texas Higher Education Coordinating Board (Spring, 2000) cited the college for outstanding developmental education program data collection. Finally, Richland College is one of only a handful of colleges nationally using the *NADE Self-Evaluation Guides* to evaluate its programs. NADE has certified Richland as a Distinguished Developmental Education Provider.

In addition, the college has approximately five years of data on the following:

- TASP pass rates after remediation (local and state comparative data and indicators)

- Graduation rates for students who were enrolled in developmental education courses

- Student performance on exit exams in developmental reading and developmental writing capstone courses

- Course completion and success rates in developmental math, reading, and writing courses

- Success in next-level college math and English courses and in various other college-level courses, including technical and occupational courses

- Cost effectiveness

- Student and advisor perceptions of developmental education programs and services obtained through focus groups and surveys

SPECIAL FEATURES

- Courses are offered in a variety of instructional modes including traditional lecture, self-paced laboratory, computer-based, online, learning communities, and a variety of instructional delivery options including regular semester-length, weekend, fast-track, and open enrollment formats.

- A mandatory yearlong orientation program is required of all new faculty and staff.

- A mandatory professional development program (20 hours each year) is required of all full-time faculty and staff; it includes diversity and student success and retention strategy training.

- Uniform exit standards are used in developmental courses.

- An active cross-functional Developmental Education Effectiveness Team has worked on improving developmental education for over four years.

- Exceptional support services such as the Center for Tutoring and Learning Connections, various TRIO-funded programs, and the Multicultural Center (advising and student support center) are readily available to students.

7. Valencia Community College

Contact: Ann Puyana, Interim Vice President, Academic Affairs
College Address: P.O. Box 3028, Orlando, FL 32802
Telephone Number: (407) 582-3421
Email Address: apuyana@valencia.cc.fl.us

Structure

Valencia's College Preparatory program consists of two levels of courses each in reading, writing, and mathematics. Entering students without recent qualifying SAT or ACT scores take the Computerized Placement Test (CPT), and if their scores in these skill areas are below those required for success in college-level courses, they are mandated into the appropriate prep course and level. Students must begin their college prep sequence in their first semester of enrollment and continue until they have successfully completed the precollege requirements.

Components

Some college-level courses may be taken simultaneously with the prep courses, but many have prerequisites that preclude registration before successful completion of the prep mandates. These prerequisites were created based on evidence from the Office of Institutional Research, which indicates that students who take courses for which they are underprepared generally fail or drop out. Valencia is experimenting with linked courses, intentionally registering a student cohort simultaneously in both a college prep and college-level course, in which content and skill improvement go hand in hand with the affective benefits of cohort community. Improvement in retention is already evident.

Outcomes

Overall, research shows that students who successfully complete their mandated college prep courses perform as well in college-level courses as students who tested directly into college level. And since more than 75 percent of Valencia's first-time-in-college (FTIC) students require some remediation, it is critical to our mission to ensure a good beginning for them. They should benefit from a rigorous, supportive program that serves as a gateway, not a gatekeeper, and is an integral rather than peripheral component of Valencia's professional work. In fact, one of Valencia's strategic goals is Start Right, in which we commit to dramatic improvement in student mastery of core competencies and foundation learning outcomes that will largely govern their success, their performance in advanced collegiate studies, and their persistence to graduation. Further, the college undertakes to make this a major investment priority and the focus of much of the early effort in the Learning-Centered Initiative.

Specific resources that support college prep students include:

- A three-credit student success course, taken by nearly half of the students mandated into college prep, that focuses on study and life-management skills, as well as an extended orientation to campus and college culture

- LifeMap™, a developmental advisement system that engages students as partners in their learning success through early career exploration, educational planning, and metacognitive awareness activities (including learning-style discovery and response)

- Course-linked college prep labs for expansion of and individual practice with course content

- Student Support Centers, drop-in labs for supplemental assistance and computer study

- Tutoring services

- Learning-centered instruction, including support for faculty to develop or redesign relevant, engaging, outcomes-based curricula and practices

- Assessment/improvement cycles, micro to macro throughout the college and including both formative and summative feedback loops for improved learning–qualitative and quantitative data, classroom research to institutional research

- Full-time collegewide college-prep coordinators for math and English/EAP, who work with faculty and deans on program implementation and outcomes improvement

- Exit-level competency exams to ensure common collegewide achievement and performance criteria

EAP (ESL) Courses

Valencia also has an English as a Second Language (ESL) program, recently revised statewide to English for Academic Purposes (EAP). Philosophically, Valencia does not lump ESL students with remedial (college prep) students, recognizing that second-language exposure and practice challenges are not the same as native learning gaps. The college tries to maintain parallel tracks, each eventually leading to readiness for Composition I and other college-level courses. The EAP Program includes multiple course levels of speech, reading, writing, and grammar. Placement testing for EAP includes the CPT and Levels of English Proficiency (LOEP) tests.

As an open-door institution, Valencia Community College recognizes the potential of each person to learn; in turn, faculty and staff accept a professional responsibility to help create the circumstances for students to discover, or rediscover, and develop their learning capacities. Part of Valencia's philosophy is to claim underprepared students as its own—as adult learners integrated from day one into the life and rigor of the college. The college cares as much about the core competencies of a Valencia graduate as any temporary skill gaps, as much about longterm career and educational plans as next semester's schedule.

While Valencia has demonstrated significant improvement in the persistence and success rates of the college prep students, the college continues to strive for even better results. In particular, Valencia hopes to be able to report no difference in achievement and completion rates across the diversity of the student population. At the present time, African-American and Hispanic students encounter less success in completing the prep sequence than do Anglo students. Through powerful pedagogies, focused support services, engaged students, outcomes-based design, and an improvement cycle linked to substantial key evidence, Valencia looks for an even more hopeful and productive future for students who begin by taking developmental education classes.

Effective Practices

1. Community College of Baltimore County Developmental Learning Communities with Master Learners

Contact: Donna McKusick, Senior Director for Developmental Education;
Al Starr, Learning Communities Coordinator, Essex campus
College Address: 7200 Sollers Point Rd., Baltimore, MD 21222
Telephone Number: (410) 780-6109
E-Mail Address: dmckusick@ ccbc.cc.md.us; astarr@ccbc.cc.md.us

The Community College of Baltimore County offers developmental learning communities that combine a second-level developmental reading class and a general education course, such as African American History, Health 101, and Psychology 101. Under normal circumstances, reading is a prerequisite for most general education courses, but CCBC makes an exception for these learning communities for reasons described below.

During the semester before the community is offered, the instructors of the general education and reading classes meet together to align their courses. When the community is offered, the reading instructor uses the textbook from the general education course to teach students reading skills, and the two instructors meet regularly to discuss course materials and students' learning needs.

What makes the program exceptional is the addition of a master learner. Master learners are faculty or counselors who are not experts in the discipline that is being taught in the general education class. After being trained, these individuals spend the semester with the students in the general education course and act as models by attending class regularly, taking notes, completing assignments and tests, and writing papers. In addition, once a week they run a required session for the students. These sessions provide guidance in the skills and behaviors needed to be successful in the course.

Several factors make this practice effective: (1) the retention rate is very high, both during the semester and from semester to semester; (2) the developmental reading students are working with authentic texts and are motivated to succeed because it will help them with the general education class; (3) the master learner is able to provide the instructors with feedback; (4) the master learner gets to observe another instructor and learn from that individual's teaching techniques; (5) master learners discover materials they can incorporate into courses in their disciplines (e.g., a career technology instructor was able to incorporate more diversity content into his courses after he was a master learner in a pluralism course); and (6) counselors who are master learners can report to their colleagues about the difficulties of certain courses. For instance, counselors had not thought of Health 101 as a challenging course for freshmen until two of them were master learners for this course.

For three years, Community College of Baltimore County has had students complete mid-semester and end-of-semester evaluations of their learning communities. At various points, CCBC has also had faculty and master learners evaluate the program. Finally, the college has statistical evidence related to retention.

2. COMMUNITY COLLEGE OF BALTIMORE COUNTY THE PRE-COLLEGE INSTITUTE

Contact: Donna McKusick, Senior Director for Developmental Education
College Address: 7200 Sollers Point Rd., Baltimore, MD 21222
Telephone Number: (410) 285-9491
E-Mail Address: dmckusick@ccbc.cc.md.us

The Pre-College Institute is an intensive developmental program that runs during the final three weeks of August. Upper-level developmental courses in English, reading, and math are offered in daily three-hour time blocks to students who score close to the cut-off for credit courses.

One feature of the program is the attention paid to noncognitive learning. Three additional hours are built into the program to attend to these learning needs. All students come to the Student Success Center during the Institute to take the Learning Attitudes and Study Skills Inventory on the computers. The computer registers the inventories instantly, and the Director of the Student Success Center provides a 30-minute presentation on what the results mean. Then students are given a tour of all offices on campus that might be helpful to them, such as the Advising Center, the Office for Special Services (which offers help with accommodations for students with physical or learning disabilities), the TRIO Student Support Services program, the Career Center, the library, and the Honors Center. During the tour, the various directors speak to the students and distribute literature. Students are then asked to create a plan of action for the fall semester. This plan should show areas for improvement and specific actions that will address the areas. The plan is collected during the final week of the Institute and calculated into the student's grades.

Outcomes data such as pass rates, retention to the fall and spring semesters, and GPA have been collected and examined for five years. The Pre-College Institute students have scored significantly higher than their counterparts in the traditional developmental courses in all areas. In particular, the course pass rates have been very high. CCBC attributes the high pass rates to the connections and affiliations that students are able to make with each other and with faculty and staff during the Pre-College Institute.

3. Bronx Community College
City University of New York
Freshman Initiative Program

Contact: Jason Finkelstein, Director, Coordinated Freshman Program
College Address: West 181st St. and University Ave., Rm. CO 215, Bronx, NY 10453
Telephone Number: (718) 289-5138
E-Mail Address: Jason.Finklestein@BCC.CUNY.EDU

Each year the Freshman Initiative Program (FIP) serves approximately 275 entering freshmen whose ACT English and reading scores and their CUNY Mathematics Assessment Test scores indicate that they must register for at least two developmental courses of the following designations: English 01, English 02, Reading 01, Reading 02, and Math 01.

Students enroll in a block program scheduled for a five-week module, Monday through Thursday mornings between 9 a.m. and 12 noon. In the second and third five-week modules, students move to other courses in their developmental sequence. Students also enroll in OCD 01–Orientation and Career Development (0 credits, one hour per week for the 15-week semester)–and either Geography 10 or Communications 11 at three hours, three credits for the full 15-week semester.

Class size is limited to 20 students, with additional enhancements of a peer tutor or counselor in the class and tutoring outside of class. Integrating tutors into the classroom provides faculty with an additional resource to help students, and allows students a chance to get individualized attention. A proactive tutoring model is very effective with at-risk freshmen, who often will not request academic assistance.

Two designated FIP counselors teach all the FIP students in OCD, and provide individualized counseling and early intervention services. FIP students participate in a required focus group where tutors or mentors provide a structured environment for support and problem solving. Problems related to absences, lateness, and personal issues are identified, and a counseling intervention is provided. All elements of the program work together to maximize success during the period of adjustment to the college experience.

Students are able to complete two or three developmental courses via an intensive approach, focusing on one course at a time while taking a small number of college-level courses.

In CUNY, students must pass mandated standardized exit examinations to move to the next level of developmental courses. In FIP, pass rates are higher than for the comparable college courses (20 percent higher in reading, 25 percent higher in mathematics, 20 percent higher in writing courses). Depending on the faculty member, results can be higher.

Experience has shown that entering freshmen who require developmental coursework can be overwhelmed by taking several classes, one of which must be for three credits to qualify for New York State aid. An intensive module over five weeks allows students to focus on one major skill area.

Senior full-time and selected adjunct faculty teach in FIP. The program attracts faculty interested in teaching freshman students. An FIP faculty development program is in effect.

Recruitment, registration, and placement are all personalized activities and require a high degree of coordination by a number of college offices registrar, bursar, financial aid, testing, and academic departments.

Longitudinal studies have found that the retention rates for FIP students are generally better than for other students who enter BCC with similar academic backgrounds.

The CUNY Central Administration Freshman Programs budget funds additional costs related to FIP. There is no additional cost to students. The program has been found to be a cost-effective approach to assisting high-risk freshmen.

4. BRONX COMMUNITY COLLEGE
CITY UNIVERSITY OF NEW YORK
INTERSESSION WORKSHOPS

Contact: Jason Finkelstein, Director, Coordinated Freshman Program
College Address: West 181st St. and University Ave., Room CO 215, Bronx,
NY 10453
Telephone Number: (718) 289-5138
E-Mail Address: Jason.Finklestein@BCC.CUNY.EDU

Bronx Community College has developed a program of workshops designed to assist students who have not passed required developmental education courses. Workshops are offered during January and June, with a smaller program in August.

The City University of New York requires that students in developmental education pass standardized exit examinations in the higher levels and departmental examinations in the lower levels of developmental courses.

Students who have difficulty passing the exit examinations but have shown potential to pass with some additional class time can participate in an intersession workshop. Participation is not automatic, and departments have screening procedures. A workshop generally does not replace a course.

Workshops are nine or 10 days in length for three to four hours a day, depending on the subject. Workshops focus on the skills needed to pass the exit examinations. Faculty are paid an hourly rate based on their full-time or adjunct hourly compensation.

The following are factors related to the success of the workshops:

- *Faculty-Student Ratio*. Workshops have no more than 20 students. This ratio of faculty to students allows for increased interaction and a degree of individualized attention.

- *Tutoring-Integrated Workshops*. The model found most successful combines the traditional tutoring-center design with the integration of tutors into the classroom. Tutors are assigned to work with faculty in the classroom and in learning labs. This provides an opportunity for students to get to know the tutors. The tutors are integrated into classroom activities and not isolated from the content of courses.

- *Technology.* Nearly all of the workshops use computer labs to supplement classroom instruction. Either this lab instruction is built directly into the course or students are assigned to use the labs outside of class.

- *Qualified, Experienced Faculty.* Teachers in the workshops are for the most part experienced full-time faculty. Adjuncts are also selected based on their teaching experience.

- *Involvement of Academic Departments.* Chairs from the appropriate departments are involved in the planning of the program. This involvement strengthens the program.

Intersession workshops are funded as part of the allocation from the CUNY Central Office for Freshman Programs. During the 2000-2001 academic year, approximately 1,100 students participated in a workshop. There is no cost to students. The pass rates in the workshops are high, ranging from 60 to 100 percent, depending on the subject.

Intersession workshops allow students who need additional instructional time to move beyond developmental courses into major courses without repeating the full course. Significant factors in retention are the pace at which students progress toward their degrees and the availability of financial aid as students enter the later stages of their programs. Intersession workshops address these concerns.

Bronx Community College also offers specialized workshops for students who have repeatedly failed the English exit examination and must pass in order to continue with their academic program. These workshops are 20 hours in length and are usually offered during the academic year.

5. Central Piedmont Community College, Northeast Campus
ABLE Advising and Support System

Contact: Cynthia W. Johnston, Dean, Community Development
College Address: P.O. Box 35009, Charlotte, NC 28235
Telephone Number: (704) 330-6677
E-Mail Address: cynthia_johnston@cpcc.cc.nc.us

The Adult Basic Literacy Education (ABLE) program at Central Piedmont Community College delivers basic skills remediation that is learner centered and addresses the special needs of a multifaceted population. This program allows individuals to enroll at various on- and off-campus ABLE centers designed to provide learning experiences for adults whose educational achievement is less than high school. Others fall short of skills necessary to enter college-level programs and seek the necessary skills, confidence, and certification to be successful in the next level of education.

Students who enter ABLE not only have various educational goals, but also range in age from 16 to 60-plus. Students under 18 must meet individually with the Recruitment and Retention Specialist for counseling and orientation. The first requirement for admission is proof that the individual has been out of school for six consecutive months (unless the student is from a home schooling program, has a conditional release form from a public school, or is from outside the Charlotte Mecklenburg Schools System's jurisdiction). A parent's notarized signature and the superintendent's designee's signature are required on the release form. The pre enrollment release form and counseling component provide greater assurance that students will be successful in the completion of their goals.

The student is next referred to the Basic Skills Intake Center, located on the central campus, where she takes an initial reading and math pretest, CASAS. The test is processed within a few days and the scores returned to the intake center. The intake staff contacts the student to ensure that she has the necessary paperwork of pretest scores and release forms needed to enroll.

The student is referred to the ABLE lab setting that would be most appropriate for her, based on the initial test scores and the convenience of the ABLE lab location.

A prospective student entering the ABLE lab is interviewed by the instructor, the staff, or both to determine the student's reason for attendance, and then advised about benefits that might be gained from participation. Any pretest scores or release information is documented and placed in each student's file.

Long-range goals

- Improving basic skills to become a productive member of society
- Passing the General Educational Development (GED) test
- Enrolling in Adult High School (AHS) program.
- Meeting the requirements for admission into higher education or vocational training programs
- Gaining basic, vocational, and job readiness skills to obtain, upgrade, or advance employment

Lab procedures

- Academic placement based on a needs assessment in reading, math, grammar, or pre-GED using the standardized tests CASAS, TABE, or Pre-GED test
- Completion of intake forms such as registration form, Literacy Education Information System (LEIS), lab cards, and cooperative agreement form
- Attendance expectations and operational hours of lab
- Overview of the computer lab operations

Students functioning below a 4th grade reading level are matched with trained volunteer tutors who provide one-on-one instruction with guidance from the basic skills instructors. A pool of volunteer tutors is also available to assist those who need one-on-one tutoring in other subject areas. The volunteer matches the student with a tutor and establishes a weekly schedule. An ongoing rapport develops between tutor, student, instructor, and coordinator as they review progress of the tutoring sessions.

A student who has matriculated through a course or courses of study in ABLE is referred to the next step: i.e., GED testing, Adult High School, or an academic career.

6. Community College of Denver Academic Support Center

Contact: Janet White, Director
College Address: Box 204, P.O. Box 173363, Denver, CO 80217
Telephone Number: (303) 556-2497
E-Mail Address: Janet.White@ccd.cccoes.edu

Given that an overwhelming 60 percent of the CCD's students are first-generation college students—and many of those economically challenged—Community College of Denver has created a variety of learning options and support services. The Academic Support Center (ASC), housed in the Center for Educational Advancement, is an example of a best-practice effort in the area of developmental education. The ASC offers free tutoring in ESL, GED, mathematics, reading, study skills, and writing.

Three support programs are also housed in the ASC. The Special Learning Support program assists students with learning disabilities or learning needs. Through the federally funded TRIO program, Student Support Services assists first-generation, disabled, or low-income students. Disadvantaged vocational students receive tutoring, case management, advocacy, and other individualized services through the Carl Perkins-funded Vocational Tutoring Program. The center operates Monday through Saturday, 72 hours per week, and offers one-on-one tutoring, case management, peer mentoring, assessment for learning disabilities, work in small groups, or computer-assisted instruction by faculty, professional and peer tutors, and mentors.

The ASC houses 14 full-time employees (nine assigned to ASC fulltime, five assigned at 20 to 80 percent of their workload) and about 180 tutors and technical support personnel. The ASC is funded in part with dollars earned through FTE, a system of equating hours of service to regular FTE earned through student registration in classes. The balance of the funding comes from the college's general fund. The college has demonstrated a significant commitment to ensuring the success of underprepared students through this fiscal allocation.

The labs and programs in the Academic Support Center serve as an integral part of the developmental education curriculum. Full- and part-time, mostly developmental faculty tutor in the drop-in labs, along with professional and peer tutors. Faculty incorporate into their curricula computerized assignments using software housed in the ASC and require students to attend the appropriate lab at least one hour weekly. Lab coordinators are selected from existing full-time developmental faculty to ensure that lab activities support and enhance classroom instruction. Tutor training programs and regular evaluation of employees and services help ensure the quality of the center.

The ASC serves an average of 56 percent of the college student population each fall and spring semester for a headcount of between 3,800 and 4,000 students (duplicated headcount is about 6,800). The ASC serves students from the Community College of Denver (all campuses), Metropolitan State College, and the University of Colorado in Denver. The hours of service to students during a typical fall or spring semester come to approximately 55,000. Students served by the ASC average about a 90 percent success rate in classes for which they receive support. Students rated tutors as "outstanding," a 4.79 composite score on a scale of 1 to 5.

7. DES MOINES AREA COMMUNITY COLLEGE ACADEMIC SKILLS GUIDE

Contact: Sue Wickham, Academic Achievement Center Instructor
College Address: 2006 S. Ankeny Blvd., Ankeny, IA 50021
Telephone Number: (515) 965-7000
E-Mail Address: smwickham@dmacc.cc.ia.ua

The *Academic Skills Guide* is a Web-based resource identifying the entry-level reading, language, math, learning, and computer skills needed for success in each diploma and degree program offered at Des Moines Area Community College. Each subject area includes a general description of the skills needed, with an explanation of how they are used both in the program and on the job. Links are provided from the subject areas to detailed skills grids (e.g., multiplying fractions, using metric measurements, reading charts and graphs). Links are also provided to related programs grouped by career clusters.

The *Skills Guide* bridges the information gap between skills testing and program expectations, allowing prospective students to understand why they need to build strong academic skills in order to be successful in the careers they have chosen.

Creating the *Skills Guide* required cooperation across the institution. Academic deans encouraged program chairs to participate in the interview process. An Internet marketing specialist in the college's Marketing and Media Relations department designed templates for each of the three Web pages needed. Academic Achievement Center faculty receive release time to create survey instruments, interview program chairs, compile the results in a readable format, and enter the data on the templates.

In previous incarnations, the *Academic Skills Guide* was formatted as a booklet. Uploading this information to the Web makes it accessible to the broadest possible population, including DMACC counselors and advisors, high school counselors and teachers, social service agencies, and prospective students. The Web format is also easy to update, as department chairs now review it annually for accuracy.

A sample *Skills Guide* entry for the Accounting Information Systems program can be viewed at http://www.dmacc.cc.ia.us/skillsguide/a-accntgis.htm.

8. Glendale Community College
Maricopa Community College District
Collegewide Assessment Initiative

Contact: Charles F. Jeffery, Associate Dean of Instruction
College Address: 6000 West Olive Ave., Glendale, AZ 85302
Telephone Number: (623) 845-3698
E-Mail: charles.jeffery@gcmail.maricopa.edu

In 1998, Glendale Community College initiated a program to assess the academic achievement of its graduates. This program uses quantitative measures to obtain information about student learning and has focused on three core outcomes: writing, critical reading, and critical reasoning (including mathematics). These core outcomes mirror the Maricopa Governing Board goals. The Governing Board has also articulated several secondary goals that will be addressed as the program matures.

Glendale Community College chose The Academic Profile as its instrument for assessment. This nationally normed test is intended for use by colleges and universities and presents students with questions from three academic areas: humanities, social sciences, and natural sciences. In addition, this test measures college-level reading, writing, critical thinking, and mathematics skills.

The Academic Profile is offered to a randomly selected number of students graduating with an associate degree. Invitations are mailed in March of each year. Instructions to the faculty, second invitations, and telemarketing complete the process to obtain a cohort representative of the GCC graduating class. Assessment is conducted during an entire week, 12 hours per day, in a central venue.

The 2000-2001 assessment provided results that reflected performance of the GCC cohort population within a margin of error of ±8 percent. GCC students scored above the national mean in all assessment areas, in the top 3 percent of all Associate of Arts college sophomores, and in the top 24 percent of all sophomores from universities and liberal arts colleges using this instrument.

Several features have emerged over the last three years that have contributed to assessment successes at GCC. First, faculty are inextricably linked to assessment. They participate in the invitation process, proctor the instrument, are informed of all outcomes, and review and critique the entire process each year. Second, faculty and administrators encourage students to participate and to do their very best. To that end, the college waives participating students' cap-and-gown rental fees and provides a letter from the dean of instruction or president for students who score in the top 25 percent and 10 percent, respectively. Third, lessons from assessment at the collegewide level are shared at annual convocations, in working groups, and with department liaison personnel to improve parallel initiatives in program and course-level assessment.

Outcome data are available for academic years 1998-1999, 1999-2000, and 2000-2001. More detailed reports on assessment at Glendale Community College can be obtained from Charles F. Jeffery, Associate Dean of Instruction (623) 845-3698, or Linda Hawbaker, Director of Institutional Effectiveness (623) 845-3560. Annual reports are produced each year for the Maricopa County Community College District and Governing Board, and incorporated in an annual districtwide report.

9. Holyoke Community College Learning Communities for Students in Developmental Education Courses

Contact: Hannah S. Gray, Dean of Academic Support
College Address: 303 Homestead Ave., Holyoke, MA 01040
Telephone Number: (413) 552-2577
E-Mail Address: hgray@hcc.mass.edu

Learning Communities (LCs) at Holyoke Community College (HCC) have a rich history. Initiated in the early 1990s, they took off in 1994 when a FIPSE grant helped to accelerate their growth. Since then, HCC Learning Communities have become a national model. At the same time, LCs specifically for developmental students have evolved as an effective educational practice as well. They include the following configurations: English 096; English 099; LCs composed of one or two developmental education courses (English or math) and/or one transfer credit course and LCs made up of linked courses (two, three, and occasionally four). Approximately 12 LCs per year are offered to 240 developmental students–nearly 20 percent of students who test into developmental courses.

English 096 is a six-credit course combining developmental writing and developmental reading; a single instructor teaches the course. A community is formed, through the integration of the content in the two courses and the collaborative learning activities, for 20 or fewer students during six class hours per week. One section of English 096 is currently linked with Introduction to Criminal Justice, and a retention specialist advises, counsels, and provides other kinds of support services to the group. In addition, a professional tutor provides five hours of tutoring per week.

English 099 also is a six-credit course for students who need developmental writing and reading. The course is team-taught by one instructor from the English department and one from another discipline such as history, anthropology, sociology, or business. The course is centered on a theme taken from the non-English discipline–for example, the Civil Rights Movement–and presents reading and writing skills as part of the course content. Academic support is offered to students in a variety of formats: individual tutoring by appointment, study group, or walk-in assistance in the writing center.

Six English 099s have been offered over the last two years at Holyoke Community College. So far, students and faculty are enthusiastic about this approach to developmental education. Team teaching encourages collaboration, creativity, and critical thinking in the classroom, and presents faculty as learning role models for the students. However, the faculty are reviewing the practice of using a single grade for English 099 since they believe one grade does not accurately reflect the student's performance when the achievement measures in reading and writing are markedly different.

Other learning communities have included Fundamentals of Writing or Reading Efficiency in combination with basic math and introductory-level psychology, biology, or philosophy, for a total of six credits. These were part of a pioneering, collegewide initiative in which faculty developed learning communities of one humanities and one science or math course to help bridge the two disciplines. While some of these developmental LCs had limited success, college faculty continue to explore new course combinations and new support strategies to increase student academic progress.

Linked courses have provided an effective learning community for developmental students. Students sign up for a block of courses–usually two, but sometimes three or even four–which they attend together. The faculties consult informally with each other, and also with support program staff, when the students are experiencing difficulty in one or more courses. The faculty and staff then determine the appropriate strategies to provide the students with academic help, such as a study group, individual tutoring, computer-aided instruction, or workshops on study skills.

The STRIVE (SSS/TRIO) Program at HCC links Reading, Fundamentals of Writing, Sociology, and I.D.E.A.S., our College Success course. The courses may have a common theme but are taught independently. Two study groups led by a professional tutor are offered for sociology and for reading and writing. Students are strongly urged to attend, and many do. A service-learning option is also available to students in the STRIVE LC.

The practices described above are being evaluated by members of the Developmental Education (DE) Forum and a subgroup, the DE Implementation Team. The Forum is an advisory body formed to increase collaboration among developmental educators and support staff, to review current practices, and to make recommendations. The Forum, composed of faculty, professional staff, tutors, and administrators, has encouraged the development of LCs, the integration of some form of academic support into the LCs, and collaboration among faculty, support staff, and administrators. More instructors are volunteering to teach LCs, and the models continue to be refined. Research on student retention, persistence, grade point average, and satisfaction related to developmental LCs has been initiated. Committed faculty and staff will use the research as well as their own experiences to direct the robust future of Learning Communities for Developmental Education at Holyoke Community College.

10. Madison Area Technical College Learning to Learn Camp

Contact: Karen Anderson, Science Instructor
College Address: 3550 Anderson St., Madison, WI 53704
Telephone Number: (608) 246-6496
E-Mail Address: klanderson@madison.tec.wi.us

A *Learning to Learn Camp* is an intensive one-week experience with a primary outcome to challenge and inspire students to grow and develop skills essential for their success in college. To successfully complete the camp, learners must meet five camp goals:

- Enhance personal discovery and self-awareness.
- Grow assessment skills in order to foster personal responsibility for learning.
- Strengthen habits for time and career management.
- Build teaming skills and be able to function within a learning community.
- Build essential skills for a learned person.

Students spend the week in learning communities and, in teams, attend classes in order to complete activities chosen to complement the five camp goals. As a result of experiencing both successes and failures during the week, participants gain confidence in their self-assessment abilities, learning where their strengths lie and in what areas they need to improve. Coaches mentor students to help foster this greater sense of learner ownership, self-esteem, and empowerment.

The camp also offers an exceptional staff development opportunity for both teaching staff and non teaching staff by acknowledging the skills each member brings. The coaches work individually and in teams to mentor student growth. During the week, much reflection takes place on the teaching and learning processes coaches use with their students. Coaches are also encouraged to give feedback on each other's performances, thus modeling the active process of real-time assessment to the students.

We have evidence to show some success in a staff goal, which is to improve student retention and course completion rates for those enrolled in the camp. We are working to better integrate the camp with current student success initiatives within the college. Our hope is that the camp complements a movement toward learning community cohorts; in which groups of students stay together during the semester; with faculty and peer mentors so that continuous, real-time assessment and student success can be achieved.

11. MORAINE VALLEY COMMUNITY COLLEGE LEARNING DEVELOPMENTAL SUPPORT SYSTEM

Contacts: Toula Karnavas, Associate Professor of Developmental Education and Instructional Coordinator; Debbie Sievers, Director of Center for Disability Services
College Address: 10900 S. 88th Ave., Palos Hills, IL 60465
Telephone Number: (708) 974-4300
E-Mail Addresses: karnavas@moraine.cc.il.us and sievers@moraine.cc.il.us

Learning Development Support System (LDSS) is designed to help students with learning disabilities and attention disorders to succeed at the college level. LDSS offers compensatory tools to assist students with their individual learning weaknesses. The program offers small-group orientation sessions for incoming students to ensure that they understand college programs, services, and degree requirements. Diagnostic evaluation and review are also offered. A diagnostician is available to administer cognitive-ability and achievement tests. A professional staff is then scheduled to evaluate the test results and select appropriate accommodations for the student.

Personal counseling, career exploration, and educational advising are available to students. Each semester, high school juniors and seniors with disabilities are invited to visit Moraine Valley. They attend a presentation offered by the staff from the Center for Disability Services, and as part of the presentation a Moraine Valley student with a disability speaks to the group about his or her college experiences. In addition, the Transition Network Committee—staff from the Center for Disability Services, high school special education teachers, and counselors—meets twice each semester to share information and coordinate services to better prepare the high school students for college.

LDSS assists students in the classroom by selecting appropriate accommodations to compensate for the students' learning weaknesses. Accommodations include extended testing time, tape recorders, note takers, enlarged print materials, test proctoring, scribes, and preferential seating.

Each semester the instructional coordinator notifies faculty of the students' services and accommodations; furthermore, the instructional coordinator is available to help adapt instruction to students' individual needs. Free tutoring is available in the Academic Skills Center. Every effort is made to schedule individual tutoring, and some individual tutoring is offered at a new computer lab designed exclusively for students with disabilities. Software is available to assist students with dyslexia and other visual and auditory discrimination deficits.

The academic success of students in the LDSS program is monitored in a number of ways. Each semester, the instructional coordinator mails midterm progress forms to faculty. The feedback reveals which students are at risk for academic failure, and appropriate steps can be taken to assist those students. In addition, the number of tutoring hours is calculated each semester for those students using the Academic Skills Center. Furthermore, each semester the students' grade point averages are compared to the grade point averages of the general student population. LDSS encourages and enhances academic, career, and personal growth in a diverse student population.

Over half of the new students receiving services through LDSS begin their college experience in developmental education. They need encouragement in using the compensatory tools available to them.

12. Piedmont Technical College Developmental and Transitional Studies Department General Education and Transitional Studies Division

Contact: Donna Foster, Department Chairperson; Jane Rauton, Dean GETS
College Address: P.O. Drawer 1467, 620 North Emerald Rd., Greenwood,
            SC 29648
Telephone Number: College (864) 941-8324
            Department: (864) 941-8430
E-Mail Address: foster_d@piedmont.tec.sc.us

The Developmental and Transitional Studies Department is organized in the General Education and Transitional Studies Division of Piedmont Technical College. Piedmont Technical College is an open-door institution. Applicants for admission must meet the following requirements:

- Be at least 18 years of age

- Possess a high school diploma or GED, or earn acceptable scores on ASSET or COMPASS placement tests or SAT

- Demonstrate the ability to benefit from formal education

Placement into developmental and transitional studies courses is not mandatory. After receiving scores on the placement instrument, the student meets with an academic advisor to determine the best direction of study.

The academic advising system at Piedmont Technical College is well designed. Students are assigned to a faculty advisor. The student is asked to sign a waiver if he chooses not to enroll in the developmental courses suggested by the placement-test interpretation.

Both developmental and transitional courses are offered, with one level of developmental coursework and one level of transitional coursework. The following courses are offered:

Mat 041	Developmental Mathematics
Rdg 041	Developmental Reading
Eng 041	Developmental English
Mat 100	Introduction to College Math
Rdg 100	Critical Reading
Eng 100	Introduction to Composition
Col 103	College Skills
Mat 101	Beginning Algebra

The Beginning Algebra course provides a brush-up on algebra for students who have taken algebra in high school or an earlier college experience, but whose placement scores indicate a beginning algebra course is needed.

Piedmont Technical College offers the following support for all students:

- *Tutoring.* Students may sign up for one free hour of tutoring per week in one course. Additional tutoring can be provided, but there is a charge.

- *Academic Advantage.* One of the federally-funded TRIO programs serves at-risk students. This program provides counseling, extra tutoring, cultural awareness trips to students who qualify for the program, and college trips to qualified students planning to continue their education beyond the technical college level.

- *Computer-Assisted Instruction in an Open Lab Setting.* Students experiencing difficulties with math, reading, and English can access a variety of software packages to help strengthen their areas of weakness. A teaching assistant is available.

- *Coordinators or Other Full-Time Faculty Members.* These professionals hold open lab time (three hours per week) to assist students with coursework in developmental and transitional studies courses.

- *Student Success Center.* This center houses student support services such as counseling, career planning and job placement, single parent grant counseling, ADA counseling, and minority retention counseling.

The college reports data to the Commission on Higher Education and the South Carolina Department of Education. This data includes completion information, withdrawal information, tracking of open-lab usage, student evaluation of faculty, grade distribution, and tracking of tutoring. In addition, the department generates other data as needed for research.

On the Lander University Campus, Piedmont Technical College provides developmental education instruction in math, reading, and English to students who do not place into freshman courses. Piedmont Technical College operates county centers in each of the seven counties in its service area. In four of these centers, a one-room school concept is used to teach developmental studies courses. The same full-time instructor teaches the courses: math, reading, and English. Student composition may change, as not all students need all three courses.

The Developmental and Transitional Studies department offers several Internet courses. Mat 041, Mat 100, Col 103 and Eng 100 are offered via the Internet. Completion rates are competitive with other Internet offerings at the college.

All developmental courses are supported by Internet-based software that can be accessed from any location. Students complete one hour of computer lab outside of class each week. They may work on campus or off campus. The software used is Skillstutor and Interactive Math.

Factors Contributing to Effectiveness

The Developmental and Transitional Studies Department is effective thanks to its well-respected and dedicated faculty, college support, and student support services. The developmental and transitional studies faculty members are well-credentialed. All full-time instructors have at least a master's degree in their fields and teach curriculum-level courses from time to time. Several of the department members have received teaching awards such as South Carolina Governor's Professor of the Year, the David Pierce Faculty Learner-Centered Quality Award, and the Freshman Experience Teaching Award. Several faculty members are participants in the South Carolina Technical College System Advanced Technical Education Exemplary Faculty Grant, funded by the National Science Foundation.

Faculty members have been National Science Foundation grants, Cooper Power PACE grants, and South Carolina Commission of Higher Education Distance Education grants.

The department is housed with the general education faculty. This promotes excellent communication and respect for job duties. All full-time faculty are members of the South Carolina Association for Developmental Educators (SCADE), and many are members of the National Association for Developmental Education. Several members have held leadership roles in state professional organizations.

The college respects the work of the faculty. Faculty in developmental and transitional studies are actively involved in the work of the college. Many serve on central college committees and task forces, and one member of the department is a faculty mentor. The faculty is experienced and enjoys teaching developmental students. Faculty members support students by offering sessions on self-help topics during the semester. Examples of these include how to study math, how to operate a calculator, and how to study science. Coordinators or instructors hold drop-in help sessions for all students enrolled in a developmental course.

The college supports the work of the developmental and transitional department. Needs receive attention and support from the divisional dean, a former developmental instructor, and other faculty members in the division. Many of the general-education faculty members teach courses for the developmental and transitional studies department. Admissions, student records, financial aid, and other college departments work closely with the department. At Piedmont, everyone works together to ensure student success.

Another reason the department is effective is the depth of student support services available at Piedmont. The college has three full-time counselors in the Student Success Center. One counselor works primarily with developmental students and minority male retention. The college has an ADA counselor who works with the department to identify disabilities and provide services to students in need of assistance.

Academic Advantage, a TRIO program, helps students adapt to the college environment and provides academic assistance. There is an open lab, staffed with several teaching assistants, which is dedicated to providing assistance to developmental and transitional students. In addition to this lab, the college has a writing center to assist all students. The tutoring center provides free and paid tutoring to students. Our instructors work with all of these services to provide the support students need to be productive and successful in college.

13. NORTHWEST VISTA COLLEGE COOPERATIVE LEARNING LAB FOR MATHEMATICS

Contact: Julie Pace, Academic Leader of Math, English, and Reading
College Address: 3535 N. Ellison Dr., San Antonio, TX 78251
Telephone Number: (210) 348-2250
E-mail Address: pace@accd.edu

Northwest Vista College (NVC) is an innovative institution that is exploring cooperative learning techniques as well as the use of learning communities. The Cooperative Learning Lab for Mathematics is a required lab (one hour per week) for all developmental math students. Students are encouraged to come to the lab with their cooperative group, established in the lecture portion of the course.

There are four levels of developmental math at NVC. Students from all four levels attend the lab during any single hour, but are segregated by level. During the typical lab hour, one lab instructor and one tutor handle the 35 or so students attending. The students work on assignments from their lecture classes, on TASP (Texas State Academic Skills Program) reviews, or on a lab curriculum written by the math faculty. The lab counts for 10 percent of a student's lecture grade. This lab portion of the grade is based solely on the number of times the student attends.

NVC has a high retention rate in developmental math, attributable to the sense of community the lab provides for the students.

SPECIAL FEATURES

- Grades are based on attendance.

- Cooperative learning is required in the lab.

- The lab emphasizes study and developmental skills as well as math skills.

- TASP skills are enhanced.

- The groups in the lab comprise miniature learning communities.

FACTORS CONTRIBUTING TO EFFECTIVENESS

- The cooperative nature of the lab builds community. Some cooperative groups extend from semester to semester.

- Students get some relief from math anxiety. They are better learners because they have the hands-on experience of teaching each other.

- Many more students are exposed to quality interactive time.

Most classes at NVC are taught using cooperative learning techniques. All developmental courses (math, English, reading) have cooperative learning labs. The Cooperative Learning Lab for Math is an extension of a very innovative learning environment at NVC.

14. Seattle Central Community College Learning Communities: Coordinated Studies Program

Contact: Audrey Wright
College Address: 1701 Broadway Ave., Seattle, WA 98020
Telephone Number: (206) 587-3800

Coordinated studies is a form of learning-community pedagogy designed to let students discover the connection and interrelatedness of disciplines and knowledge. A learning community is one in which students and faculty members accept the role and the responsibility of being learners. It typically uses two to four faculty teaching their respective disciplines to a cohort of students who have enrolled in 10 to 18 credits of discipline content organized around a theme.

While the practice usually involves college- or university-level content, these developmental applications have been designed to include precollege content. Some examples are Bite of Seattle, which offers developmental English along with college-level history; Building for College Success, which includes ESL and computer literacy; and Business, Power, & Communication, which includes developmental English and math, along with Business 100. A successful preparatory application for pre-allied health programs is titled Health Connection: Learning for Success. It includes Science 100 and Introduction to Chemistry, Biology, and Anatomy, along with developmental math and English.

As with the college-level coordinated studies, the retention rate for coordinated studies programs that contain developmental courses has uniformly exceeded 90 percent. Research by Vincent Tinto and others indicates that students find coordinated education interesting and relevant (Tinto, Love, & Russo, 1994).

English as a Second Language Program

1. COMMUNITY COLLEGE OF DENVER

Contact: Ruth Brancard, ESL Program Chair
College Address: CB 600, P.O. Box 173363, Denver, CO 80217
Telephone Number: (303) 556-3886
E-Mail Address: ruth.brancard@ccd.ccoes.edu

The English as a Second Language Program (ESL) at the Community College of Denver (CCD) serves approximately 500 students per semester, with a growth rate of 68 percent in the past five years. Most of the students are immigrants and refugees who are making Colorado their home. They are a very diverse group, representing approximately 40 countries and ranging in age from 17 to 70. Their educational goals vary. After ESL classes, many continue their studies to complete vocational certificates, associate's degrees, and bachelor's degrees, while a few continue for advanced degrees. Some are taking English to improve their chances for job advancement.

The academic preparation strand of the ESL program is part of the Center for Educational Advancement that houses developmental programs in English, reading, and math. The ESL program offers basic, intermediate, and advanced classes in grammar, reading, composition, and conversation, as well as special classes in spelling and pronunciation, with the goal of preparing students to do academic work in English. Upon application to the college, students are tested in CCD's test center and are recommended to courses based on those test results. Students follow a course sequence through the program, taking developmental reading and English courses if tests show they need them. Students at advanced levels may begin coursework in math, computer applications, or other subjects as appropriate.

Post-tests in reading and grammar classes allow checks for program effectiveness. Data from 1993-1998 show retention rates for ESL students are higher than overall college rates. Retention rates from fall-to-spring averaged 72.63 percent, as compared with 60.48 percent for all students.

Fall-to-fall retention rates were at 71.90 percent. Eighty-five percent of ESL students attempting English 121 Freshman Composition completed the course with a grade of C or better, compared to 71 percent of students who had taken developmental courses and 69 percent of students who had not taken developmental courses.

Distinctive features that contribute to the program's success include tutoring support through the ESL lab in the Academic Support Center, semi-intensive integrated language skills classes at the basic and intermediate levels, highly interactive instructional approaches in most classes, and flexible scheduling mornings, evenings, and weekends. Other keys to success are instructors with experience and education in teaching ESL, a well-defined curriculum, and a collegewide commitment to serving this diverse student population.

2. El Paso Community College

Contact: Dennis E. Brown, Vice President of Instruction
Address: P.O. Box 20500, El Paso, TX 79998
Telephone number: (915) 831-5211
E-Mail Address: dennisb@epcc.edu

The Developmental Education Program has two components: basic academic skills and content-based remediation. In addition, the college offers a comprehensive English as a Second Language Program (ESL). The Basic Academic Skills program (BASK) works with students in writing, reading, mathematics, and study skills at the basic-literacy skill level up to the beginning secondary level. Content-based remediation carries the student through the secondary level in the three skill areas. The content-based courses are offered directly though the English, reading, and mathematics disciplines so that students can smoothly transition into college-level courses in these skill areas. The English as a Second Language Program brings students up to the collegiate level so they can perform successfully in a college classroom. The ESL student may also benefit from study skills and mathematics courses offered through the Developmental Education Program.

The BASK program has two writing courses, one reading course, two math courses, and two study-skills courses. The content-based remedial offerings include two writing courses, three reading courses, and three math courses. The ESL program has six levels and 24 courses. Students entering the developmental courses are placed using the Descriptive Test of Language Skills and Conventions, the Descriptive Test of Language Skills and Reading Comprehension, and the Descriptive Test of Math Skills. An alternate testing instrument is the Accuplacer. Instructional support labs are available for all of the above offerings, and include individual and group tutoring, computer-assisted instruction, and other forms of assistance.

The college is just completing its first year using the SCT Banner system, and data are now being compiled that can be used to assess outcomes of developmental and ESL students. Data in the Legacy system is outdated and in some cases no longer available.

A feature of the developmental education program is the blending of basic remediation training offered through the BASK program with the transitional remediation offered through the content disciplines of English, reading, and math. The comprehensive nature of the ESL program, which takes students from no English language skills to college-level performance, is the distinctive feature. A successful component of the ESL program is English for Specific Purposes, where students acquire both English skills and content (e.g., child development, computers) simultaneously.

The developmental programs are effective because they integrate a strong developmental curriculum with a transitional remedial curriculum that allows the student to advance into college-level writing and math courses in a logical sequence. Complementing the strong curriculum is a talented cadre of developmental faculty who have both the desire to work with these students and the insight into the teaching-learning process for students needing remedial instruction. The ESL program is effective because it is comprehensive (writing, reading, speaking, and listening), logically sequenced, and taught by a core group of talented and experienced faculty.

3. WILLIAM RAINEY HARPER COLLEGE

Contact: Wallis Sloat, Co-chair, ESL/Linguistics Department and International Student Office
College Address: 1200 W. Algonquin Rd., Palatine, IL 6006
Telephone Number: (847) 925-6717
E-Mail Address: wsloat@harper.cc.il.us

The ESL/Linguistics Department and International Student Office is a part of the Academic Enrichment and Language Studies Division of Harper College. Under the direction of two co-chairs who report to the division dean, the department offers two programs of instruction for students whose native language is not English and who are able to read and write in their first language. Students pay the college tuition rate or the international rate, depending on their status.

The part-time academic program, serving 1,100 to 1,200 students each fall and spring semester, includes a core sequence of six integrated-skills courses. Their purpose is to provide comprehensive instruction in English for students who are able to study only four hours per week. In addition, the part-time program offers courses in reading, writing, and grammar at five levels ranging from beginning to advanced. Students who attain a B or A average in the advanced reading and writing courses are qualified to take English 101, the college requirement for an associate's degree. Finally, the program offers vocabulary, pronunciation, American culture, and TOEFL preparation classes for high-intermediate to advanced students. In the shortened summer session, Part-Time Program students may take conversation and spelling courses suited to their level.

The Intensive English Program is accredited by the Commission on English Language Accreditation. It consists of 18 hours of classroom instruction per week for three 12-week sessions per year and serves approximately 150 full-time students each session. The four levels range from beginning to high-intermediate, after which the students transfer to the Part-Time Program to complete the advanced courses. Each level of study includes reading, writing, listening, speaking, conversation, and grammar.

Students enrolled in this program also work independently in the ESL language laboratory for at least one hour per week.

Student support services include registration, tutoring, language-lab or computer services, and advising. Scores on reading, writing, and grammar-speaking tests determine placement of new students. Progression through the courses is dependent on the instructor's assessment and, in the case of writing classes, a department exit assessment exam. Adjunct faculty members provide half-hour tutoring sessions for at-risk students referred by their classroom instructors. A fully staffed language laboratory is available for students to improve listening and pronunciation skills via study units prepared by the ESL lab supervisor. Computers with interactive ESL software are located in the lab and in the ESL computer classroom. The main purpose of the 24-station computer classroom, however, is to provide computer-assisted instruction to intermediate and advanced writing students, whose classes meet there regularly. Finally, three ESL advisors–two of whom are fully trained in international student issues–provide academic and career guidance, immigration information, and limited personal counseling. Upon arrival at Harper, the international students receive an orientation to the college, including information about insurance, campus activities, and personal health and safety concerns. In addition, one advisor sponsors a mentoring program pairing U.S. students with international students to encourage cultural information exchanges and lifelong friendships.

The effectiveness of these two programs arises from class size, which is limited to 20, and from the range of courses available. It is thus possible to address a variety of needs, from those of the employed, resident population seeking to improve one or two skill areas, to the young immigrant beginning a college or vocational career. The strongest indication of program effectiveness is the continuing demand of community members and international students for classes. In addition, research done by the college in 1997 indicated that successful completion of the ESL advanced reading and writing courses is the highest predictor of student success in college-level English courses.

The department has 11 full-time tenure-track instructors, all of whom participate in different facets of the programs, including curriculum review, textbook selection, mentoring of adjunct faculty, and testing and placement of students. In addition, these faculty serve on institutional committees and can influence policy decisions impacting ESL students. Approximately 40 adjunct faculty are employed each semester; new hires are mentored and evaluated by the program coordinator for two semesters, after which they are evaluated by full-time faculty peers once every three years. In addition, students evaluate full-time faculty once a year and adjuncts each semester, and they have given faculty high ratings. In summary, the success of the department can be attributed to the quality and size of its faculty and staff and its integration in the college, which has provided considerable support.

4. RICHLAND COMMUNITY COLLEGE

Contact: Jean Conway, Dean, World Languages, Cultures, and
        Communications
College Address: 12800 Abrams Rd., Dallas, TX 75243
Telephone Number: (972) 238-6943
E-Mail Address: jconway@dcccd.edu

The mission of the Richland College ESOL program is to develop the comprehensive English language skills of non-native English speakers through dynamic, innovative instruction in reading, writing, oral communication, and cross-cultural interaction, which facilitates the achievement of their learning goals for college-level academic courses as well as in career and community environments. Designed to accommodate the geographic, linguistic, and cultural diversity of students scattered across a large urban county, the ESOL model is incorporated into the strategic planning and learning programs of the college. The program is housed within an academic division where it shares equal status with other college language programs. Consistent program evaluation allows fluid transformation and improvement with maximum consideration for students' needs and preferences.

In response to the diverse needs of these students, Richland College offers ESOL courses to prepare students for success in college-level courses through learning communities, discrete skill classes, and the American English and Culture Institute, as well as workforce and social language acquisition through continuing education. Learning communities link the four discrete language skill areas in a thematic approach. Two proficiency levels are offered each fall and spring semester in an intensive, fast-track mode.

Discrete skill classes include focused learning in listening and speaking, reading, writing, and grammar, plus individualized lab components to supplement classroom instruction. Four proficiency levels of instruction are offered from high-beginning through advanced.

The American English and Culture Institute provides an intensive fast-track English program for international students (students on an F-1 visa) in a year-round program of eight-week sessions. This program consists of six proficiency levels of instruction–beginning through advanced–and includes a culture-studies component at every level.

A continuing education program offers courses to assist students in improving their English skills for the workplace or in social situations. Individual courses are taught with an integrated skills approach at seven proficiency levels–preliteracy through advanced–in both semester and intensive, fast-track formats. Delivery of instruction is made available on campus and is customized for worksites throughout the community.

The admission of ESOL students carries with it an ethical responsibility to provide a full range of student services consistent with the needs of this special population. The ESOL programs at Richland College take a holistic approach to fully meeting student goals in both academic and life arenas. A number of student support services and assistance programs for academic success serve students as they pursue language proficiency. The Multicultural Center serves as an advising and referral center designed to meet the academic needs of ESOL students. The Center is staffed by a diverse group of student services professionals who are committed to positively impacting student learning and retention by providing high-quality, caring support services. Services include a comprehensive student intake, assessment, and placement process that assists students in identifying academic goals and selecting appropriate classes. Skilled academic advisors help students define their educational and career plans and facilitate their ongoing registration.

The Center schedules regular orientation sessions offering students detailed information about all college services and opportunities. Personal counseling and community referrals are available to ensure holistic student wellness. Academic Success Programs assist ESOL students in achieving their academic goals. The Center for Tutoring and Learning Connections furnishes opportunities for individual and independent study for students. Through a variety of learning approaches, from skill-specific interactive software to one-on-one tutoring and focused writing workshops, the Center's programs are tailored for individual student success. Every ESOL credit course includes a lab component to supplement classroom instruction. Other support programs are provided on campus such as the award-winning Conversation Partners program, in which volunteers from a community-based Emeritus program visit and talk with students. They give students regular oral practice and emotional and cultural support, as well as lasting friendship.

Life Skills Resources offer students an appropriate balance of social and intercultural interaction. This is achieved through a variety of student programs, culture- and language-specific student clubs, intercultural awareness forums, and student dialogues. ESOL students are also introduced to related community events and resources.

Richland College's pre-academic ESOL program, which has over 8,000 registrations per year, has consistently provided a strong academic base to non-native English speakers entering academic programs. All ESOL course outcomes are defined through skill-specific exit competency exams, which meet the required standards of college-level academic faculty. To demonstrate this, a fall 1999 statistical study by the Office of Institutional Research found that in designated language-intensive college-level courses, ESOL completers outperformed native English speakers. This high performance rate of ESOL students was true when compared to native English speakers who tested directly into college-level courses as well those who had completed developmental courses.

Many components contribute to the effectiveness of Richland College's ESOL program. An innovative organizational structure places ESOL instruction within an academic division where it shares equal status with all language acquisition courses, both English and foreign-language. A variety of instructional delivery models ensures student access, achievement of goals, and opportunities for student success. A deliberate focus on the holistic needs of students leads to providing a full range of comprehensive student support services as well as enhancing intercultural competence, which equips students to thrive in an increasingly global community. As programs are continually evaluated and instruction and services enhanced, this ESOL model will continue to achieve its goals in meaningful ways and result in increasing degrees of success for ESOL students.

REFERENCES

Adams, S., & Huneycutt, K. (1998). Building a Community of Learners. In D. Mollise & C. Matthews (eds.), *NADE 98* Selected Conference Papers 4. National Association for Developmental Education.

Alderman, M. K. (1990, September). Motivation for At-Risk Students. *Educational Leadership*, 27-30.

Alfred, R., et al. (1994). *Community Colleges: Core Indicators of Effectiveness*. A Report of the Community College Roundtable. Washington DC: American Association of Community Colleges.

American Association for Higher Education, American College Personnel Association, and National Association of Student Personnel Administrators. (1998, June). *Powerful Partnerships: A Shared Responsibility for Learning*. Available: www.aahe.org/assessment/joint.htm.

Anderson, E. (1985). Forces Influencing Student Persistence and Achievement. In R. L. Noel Levitz & D. Saluri (eds.), *Increasing Student Retention*. San Francisco: Jossey-Bass.

Aragon, S. (2000). *Beyond Access: Methods and Models for Increasing Retention and Learning Among Minority Students*. San Francisco: Jossey-Bass.

Astin, A. (1993). *What Matters in College? Four Critical Years Revisited*. San Francisco: Jossey-Bass.

Banta, T.W., et al. (1996). *Assessment in Practice: Putting Principles to Work on College Campuses*. San Francisco: Jossey-Bass.

Banta, T., & Kuh, G. (1998, March/April). A Missing Link in Assessment: Collaboration Between Academic and Student Affairs Professionals. *Change*, 41-46.

Boggs, G. R. (2001, August/September). The Meaning of Scholarship in Community Colleges. *Community College Journal*, 72 (1), 60.

Boyer, E. (1992, November). Curriculum, Culture and Social Cohesion. *Celebrations*.

Boylan, H. R., Bonham, B. S., & Bliss, L. B. (1997, March). Program Components and Their Relationship to Student Performance. *Journal of Developmental Education*, 20 (3), 2-8.

Boylan, H. R., Bonham, B. S., & Bliss, L. B. (1994). Characteristic Components of Developmental Programs. *Research in Developmental Education*, 11(1). Boone, NC: National Center for Developmental Education.

Boylan, H. R., Bonham, B. S., & Bliss, L. B. (1994). Who Are the Developmental Students? Research in Developmental Education, *11*(2).

Boylan, H. R., Bonham, B. S., & Bliss, L. B. (1992). *The State of the Art in Developmental Education: Report of a National Study*. Paper presented at the First National Conference on Research in Developmental Education. Charlotte, NC.

Boylan, H. R. (1996). *Levels of Summative Evaluation*. Battle Creek, MI: Kellogg Institute Lecture.

Boylan, H. R., & Saxon, P. (1998). *An Evaluation of Developmental Education in Texas Colleges and Universities*. Austin, TX: Texas Higher Education Coordinating Board.

Boylan, H. R., Bonham, B. S., & Rodriguez, L. M. (2000). What Are Remedial Courses and Do They Work: Results of National and Local Studies. *The Learning Assistance Review*, 5, 5-14.

Boylan, H. R., Bonham, B. S., Bliss, L. B., & Claxton, C. S. (1992). *The State-of-the-Art in Developmental Education: Report of a National Study*. Paper presented at the First National Conference on Research in Developmental Education. Charlotte, NC.

Boylan, H. R., Bonham, B. S., Morante, E., Bliss, L. B., Abraham, A., Ramirez, G., Anderson, J., Allen, B., & Vadillo, M. (1996). *An Evaluation of the Texas Academic Skills Program (TASP)*. Austin, TX: Texas Higher Education Coordinating Board.

Boylan, H. R., & Saxon, P. (2001). *Outcomes of Remediation Prepared for the League for Innovation in the Community College*. Boone, NC.: National Center for Developmental Education.

Boylan, H. R. (1999). Harvard Symposium 2000: Developmental Education, Demographics, Outcomes and Activities. *Journal of Developmental Education*, 23 (2), 2-8.

Brickman, A., & Stockford, M. (2000). *Building a Systematic Approach to High School and Postsecondary Success for Students: Existing Secondary-Postsecondary Collaborations*. Boston, MA: Massachusetts Community Colleges.

Brown, W., & Holtzman, W. (1967). *Survey of Study Habits and Attitudes*. New York: The Psychological Corporation.

Cartwright, P. (1996). Technology & Underprepared Students: Part One. *Change, 28* (1), 45. Available: EBSCO Academic Search Elite. (960) 315-0397. August 1, 2001.

Cartwright, P. (1996). Technology and Underprepared Students: Part Two. *Change, 28* (3), 60-63. Available: EBSCO Academic Search Elite. (960) 625-0551. August 1, 2001.

Casazza, M. E., Clark-Thayer, S., & Materniak, G. (2001). *The NADE Certification Process*.
Available: http://umkc.edu/cad/nade/nadedocs/Certproc.htm.

Casazza, M. E., & Silverman, S. L. (1996). *Learning Assistance and Developmental Education: A Guide for Effective Practice*.
San Francisco: Jossey-Bass.

Center for Supplemental Instruction. (2000). *Review of Research Concerning the Effectiveness of Supplemental Instruction from the University of Missouri-Kansas City and Other Institutions*. Unpublished manuscript.

Christ, F., Sheets, R., & Smith, K. (2000) *Starting a Learning Assistance Center*. Clearwater, FL: H & H Publishing.

Chung, C. J. (2001). Approaching Theory In Developmental Education. In D. B. Lundell & J. Higbee (eds.), *Theoretical Perspectives for Developmental Education*. Minneapolis: Center for Research on Developmental Education and Urban Literacy, General College, University of Minnesota. Available: http://www.gen.umn.edu/research/crdeul/momograph.htm

Clark-Thayer, S. (ed.). (1995). *NADE Self-Evaluation Guides: Models for Assessing Learning Assistance/Developmental Education Programs*. Clearwater, FL: H & H Publishing.

Cohen, A. M. (1992). *Perspectives on the Community College*. Washington, DC: ERIC Clearinghouse for Junior Colleges.

College Board. (1995). *Test Administration Manual for the Accuplacer*. New York: The College Board.

College Board. (2001). WritePlacer Plus. The College Board Website. Available: http://www.collegeboard.org/accuplacer/html/writeplacer.html.

College Reading and Learning Association. (2001). Requirements for Certification of Tutor Programs. Available: http://www.crla.net/T_docPack_II_Reqs.htm

College Reading and Learning Association. (2001). The International Tutor Certification Program. Available: http://www.crla.net/Certification.htm

Covey, S. R. (1992). *Principle-Centered Leadership*. New York: Simon and Schuster.

Crookston, B. (1994). A Developmental View of Academic Advising As Teaching. NACADA Journal 14, 5-9.

Cross, K. P. (2001). *Motivation . . . Er, Will That Be on the Test?* The Cross Papers, Number 5. Mission Viego, CA: League for Innovation in the Community College.

Cross, K. P. (1997). *Developing Professional Fitness Through Classroom Assessment and Classroom Research*. The Cross Papers, Number 1. Mission Viejo, CA: League for Innovation in the Community College.

Cross, K. P. (1981). *Adults as Learners*. San Francisco: Jossey-Bass.

Dempsey, J. (2000). *One Generation Helping Another: Using Retired Volunteers in a Developmental Education Program*. Paper presented at the National Conference of the Association for Community College Trustees, Nashville, TN.

Dempsey, J. (2001, September 7). Personal interview. Pinehurst, NC: Sandhills Community College.

Elder, L., & Paul, R. (2000). Critical Thinking: Nine Strategies for Everyday Life, Part II. *Journal of Developmental Education 24* (2), 38–39.

Ender, S., Winston, R., & Miller, T. (1984). *Developmental Academic Advising*. San Francisco: Jossey-Bass.

Engston, C., & Tinto, V. (1997, July-August). Working Together for Service Learning. *About Campus*, 10-15.

Finn, L. L. (1999). Learning Disabilities Programs at Community Colleges and Four-Year Colleges and Universities. *Community College Journal of Research & Practice 23* (7), 629-640. Available: EBSCO Academic Search Elite. October 25, 2001.

Flippo, R. F., & Caverly, D. C. (eds.). (1991). *Teaching Reading and Study Strategies at the College Level*. Newark, NJ: International Reading Association.

Florida Department of Education. (2001, August 30). College Level Academic Skills Test (CLAST). Available: http://www.firn.edu/doc/sas/clast/clstlc94.htm.

Gabelnick, F., MacGregory, J., Matthews, R., & Smith, B. (1990). Learning Communities: Creating Connections Among Students, Faculty and Disciplines. *New Directions for Teaching and Learning, 41*. San Francisco: Jossey-Bass.

Gardner, J. (1998). *The Changing Role of Developmental Educators in Creating and Maintaining Student Success*. Keynote address delivered at the College Reading and Learning Association Conference, Salt Lake City, UT.

Giddan, N., Creech, F., & Lovell, V. (1988). *The Inventory for Counseling and Development*. Minneapolis National Computer Systems.

Gier, T. (1994). College Reading and Learning Association's Tutor Certification Program. In M. Maxwell (Ed.), *From Access To Success* (pp. 107-108). Clearwater, FL: H & H Publishing.

Gillman, T. J. (2001, August 6). At Last, Census Data That Trivia Buffs Can Use. *Dallas Morning News*, p. 5A.

Gleazer, E. J., Jr. (1968). *This Is the Community College*. Boston: Houghton Mifflin.

Gourney, A. (1992). Tutoring Developmental Mathematics: Overcoming Anxiety and Fostering Independent Learning. *Journal of Developmental Education 15*, 10-14.

Grubb, W. N. (1998). *From Black Box to Pandora's Box: Evaluating Remedial/Developmental Education*. Paper presented at the Conference on Replacing Remediation in Higher Education, Stanford University, Palo Alto, CA.

Hankin, J. (Ed.). (1996). *The Community College: Opportunity and Access for America's First-Year Students*. Columbia, SC: University of South Carolina.

Hanse, E., & Stephens, J. (2000. September/October). The Ethics of Learner-Centered Education. *Change*, 42-47.

Hartman, H. (1990). Factors Affecting the Tutoring Process. *Journal of Developmental Education*, 14, 2-6.

Haught, P., Hill, L, Walls, R., & Nardi, A. (1998). Improved Learning and Study Inventory (LASSI) and Academic Performance: The Impact of Feedback on Freshmen. *Journal of The First-Year Experience*, 2, 25-40.

Haycock, K. (1998). School-College Partnerships. *Higher Education and School Reform*. San Francisco: Jossey-Bass.

Higbee, J. L. (2001). The Student Personnel Point of View. In D. B. Lundell & J. Higbee (Eds.) *Theoretical Perspectives for Developmental Education*. Minneapolis: Center for Research on Developmental Education and Urban Literacy, General College, University of Minnesota. Available: http://www.gen.umn.edu/research/crdeul/momograph.htm.

Hodges, D. (2001). What Psychologists Know: And What LCC Actually does to Help Students Keep Going. *The Community College Moment*, 35-37. Eugene, OR: Lane Community College.

Hodges, R. & Dochen, C. (2001). Implementing a Learning Framework Course. In J. L. Higbee (Ed.), 2001: *A Developmental Odyssey*. Boone, NC: National Association for Developmental Education.

House, J. D. (1995). Cognitive-Motivational Variables and Prior Achievement as Predictors of Grade Performance of Academically Underprepared Students. *International Journal of Instructional Media*, 22 (4), 293-305. Available: EBSCO Academic Search Elite. August 1, 2001.

Hudgins, J. L., & Williams, S. K. (1997). Seizing the Opportunity of Institutional Effectiveness. In J. E. Roueche, et al. (Eds.), *Embracing the Tiger: The Effectiveness Debate and the Community College*. Washington DC: American Association of Community Colleges.

Ignash, J. M. (1992). *ESL Population and Program Patterns in Community Colleges*. Los Angeles, CA: ERIC Clearinghouse for Junior Colleges. Available: ERIC Document Reproduction Service No. ED 353 022.

Institute of International Education (IIE). (2000). *Open Doors*. New York: NY.

J. Sargeant Reynolds Community College. (1995). *Survey of Developmental Education Practices*. Richmond, VA: Author.

Jackson, M. (2001, August 15). DISD Offering Help to Immigrant Students. *Dallas Morning News*, p. 21A.

Jewell, P. (1996). A Reasoning Taxonomy for Gifted Education. In M.T. McCann & F. Southern (Eds.), *Fusing Talents: Proceedings of the Sixth Annual Conference on Gifted Education*. The Australian Association for the Gifted and Talented. Available: http://www.nexus.edu.au/teachstud/gat/jewell2.htm. February 13, 2002.

Keimig, R. T. (1983). *Raising Academic Standards: A Guide to Learning Improvement*. ASHE-ERIC Higher Education Research Report No. 4, ED 233 669: 30-31.

Knopp, L. (1996). Remedial Education: An Undergraduate Student Profile. Research Briefs 6, 1-11. Washington, DC: *American Council on Education*.

Krist, M. & Venezia, A. (2001, September). Bridging the Great Divide Between Secondary Schools and Postsecondary Education. *Phi Delta Kappan*, 94.

Kuo, E. (2000). *English as a Second Language: Program Approaches at Community Colleges*. Los Angeles, CA: ERIC Clearinghouse for Community Colleges. Available: ERIC Document Reproduction Service No. ED 447 859.

Kuo, E. (2000). *Student Cohort Performance in TASP-Designated College-Level Courses*. Dallas, TX: Richland College, Dallas County Community College District.

Kuo, E. (1999). Analysis of ESL Course Offerings in Community Colleges. ERIC Document Reproduction Service No. Ed 427 795.

Kuo, E. (1999). Report on International Education Exchange. New York: Institute of International Education.

Lavin, D. & Hyllegard, D. (1996). *Changing the Odds: Open Admission and Life Changes of the Disadvantaged*. New Haven: Yale University Press.

League for Innovation in the Community College (1990). *Serving Underprepared Students*. Laguna Hills, CA: Author.

Levin, J. S. (2000). The Revised Institution: The Community College Mission at the End of the Twentieth Century. *Community College Review*, 28 (2), 25. Available: EBSCO Academic Search Elite. August 1, 2001.

Levison, E. M., & Ohler, D. (1996). Transition from High School to College for Students with Learning Disabilities: Needs, Assessment, and Services. *High School Journal*, 92 (1), 62-69. EBSCO Academic Search Elite. October 25, 2001.

Levitz, R., & Noel, L. (1985). Using a Systematic Approach to Assessing Retention Needs. In L. Noel, R. Levitz, & D. Saluri (Eds.), *Increasing Student Retention*. San Francisco: Jossey-Bass.

Livingston, S., & Zieky, M. (1982). *Passing Scores*. Princeton, NJ: Educational Testing Service.

Lopez, C. (1996). *Opportunities for Improvement: Advice from Consultant-Evaluators on Programs to Assess Student Learning*. Chicago: North Central Accreditation Commission on Institutions of Higher Education.

Maitland, L. E. (2000). Ideas in Practice: Self-Regulation and Metacognition in the Reading Lab. *Journal of Developmental Education*, 24 (2), 26-36.

Martino, N. L., Norris, J. A., & Hoffman, P. R. (2001). Reading Comprehension Instruction: Effects of Two Types. *Journal of Developmental Education*, 25 (1), 3.

Materniak, G., Maxwell, M., & Clark Thayer, S. (1997). *Contextual Statement: The Role of Learning Assistance Programs*. The CAS Book of Professional Standards for Education: Council for the Advancement of Standards in Higher Education. Available: http://www.cas.edu.

Maxwell, M. (1990). Does Tutoring Help? A Look at the Literature. *Research in Developmental Education*, 7, 1-5.

Maxwell, M. (1991). *Evaluating Academic Skills Programs: A Sourcebook*. Kensington, MD: M. M. Associates.

Maxwell, M. (1994). *From Access to Success*. Clearwater, FL: H&H
   Publishing.

Maxwell, M. (1997). *Improving Student Learning Skills*. Clearwater, FL: H&H
   Publishing.

McCabe, R. H. (1998). *Developmental Education: A Twenty-first Century Social
   and Economic Imperative*. Mission Viejo, CA: League for Innovation
   in the Community College.

McCabe, R. H. (2000). *No One To Waste: A Report to Public Decision-Makers
   and Community College Leaders*. Washington, DC: Community
   College Press.

McCabe, R. H. (2001). What Should We Know About Developmental
   Education? Available: www.bobmccabe.org.

McClenney, B. (2000). Remediation is Everyone's Responsibility. *Community
   College Week*, 18: 2-3.

McCusker, M. (1999). Effective Elements of Developmental Reading and
   Writing Programs. *Community College Review*, 27 (2), 93-105.
   Available: Wilson Select Plus. BEDI99032906. August 28, 2001.

McGrath, E. (2001, September 4). Colleges of the Year: Welcome Freshmen!
   Time. Available: http://www.time.com/time/2001/coy/story.html.

McKusick, D. (1999). An Analysis of Academic Literacy Tasks Required in
   Introductory Psychology Courses in Community Colleges. College
   Park, MD: University of Maryland.

McMurtie, B. (2000). How Regional Accreditors are Changing. *Chronicle of
   Higher Education XLVI* (44), A29.

Medsker, L. L., & Tillery, D. (1996). *Remedial Education at Higher Education
   Institutions*. Washington, DC: U.S. Department of Education, Office
   of Educational Research and Improvement.

Medsker, L. L., & Tillery, D. (1971). *Breaking the Access Barriers*. Berkeley,
   CA: The Carnegie Foundation for the Advancement of Teaching
   and New York: National Center for Education Statistics.

Miller, T. (Ed.). (1999). *CAS Book of Standards in Higher Education*.
   Washington, DC: Council on Advancement of Standards in Higher
   Education.

Moats, L. (2001). When Older Students Can't Read. *Educational Leadership*, 36.

Morante, E. (1989). Selecting Tests and Placing Students. *Journal of Developmental Education 13* (2), 2-6.

Morris, C. (2001). *Retention Rates of Successful SLS Students*. Information Capsule No. 2001-1C. Miami: Miami-Dade Community College.

Morris, C. (1998). *Evaluation of SLS Intervention Courses*. Institutional Research Report No. 98-09. Miami: Miami-Dade Community College.

Moss, R. L., & Young, R. B. (1995). Perceptions about the Academic and Social Integration of Underprepared Students in an Urban Community College. *Community College Review*, 22 (4), 47-62. Available: EBSCO Academic Search Elite. 9505022388. August 1, 2001.

National Association for Developmental Education (2003). http://www.nade.net/L.%20nade_store.htm.

National Center for Educational Statistics. (1996). *Remedial Education at Higher Education Institutions, Fall 1995*. Washington, DC: U.S. Department of Education, Office of Educational Research and Improvement.

National Center for Research on Teacher Learning (1994). Learning to Walk the Reform Talk: A Framework for the Professional Development of Teachers. Available: http://ncrtl.msu/edu/

Neuburger, J. (1999, Fall). Executive Board Position Page Research and Recommendations for Developmental Education and/or Learning Assistance Programs in the State of New York. *Research and Teaching in Developmental Education*, 16 (1), 5-21.

New England Association of Schools and Colleges, Inc., Commission on Institutions of Higher Education. (1992). Policy Statement on Institution Effectiveness. *Self-Study Guide*. Bedford, MA.

North Carolina Department of Community Colleges. (1999, February). *Final Report on Senate Bill 1366, Annual Review of Accountability Enhanced*. Raleigh, NC.

Nunley, C., & Gemberling, K. (1999, January). How High School/Community College Partnerships Can Boost Academic Achievement. *Community College Journal*, 23 (5), 34-38.

Nunnally, J. (1978). *Psychometric Theory*. New York: McGraw-Hill.

O'Banion, T. (1997). *A Learning College for the 21st Century*. A joint publication of the American Association of Community Colleges and the American Council on Education. Phoenix: Oryx Press.

Ofiesh, N. S., & McAfee, J. K. (2000, January/February). Evaluation Practices for College Students with LD. *Journal of Learning Disabilities*, 33 (1), 14-26. Available: EBSCO Academic Search Elite. 2683820. October 25, 2001.

Palmer, J. (1990). *Accountability Through Student Tracking: A Review of the Literature*. Washington DC: American Association of Community and Junior Colleges.

Perin, D. (2001, August/September). Making Remediation More Learner-Centered. *Community College Journal*, 53-56.

Perin, D. (1999). Using Academic-Occupational Integration to Improve Remedial Education. *Community College Journal*, 69 (5), 26-33.

Quintanilla, R. (2001, September 11). For Some, X Plus Y Won't Quite Add Up to Z – Extra Algebra Gets Variable Results. *Chicago Tribune*, 1.

Ribble, M. (2001, Spring). Redefining Basic Writing: An Image Shift from Error to Rhizome. *BWe: Basic Writing e-Journal*, 3 (1). Available: http://www.asu.edu/clas/english/composition/cbw/spring_2001_V3N1.html.

Reed, T., Makarem, K., Wadsworth, T., & Shaughnessy, M. (1994). Intellectual and Psychosocial Status of Remedial Students. *Perceptual and Motor Skills*, 78, 249-250.

Roeuche, J. E., & Roeuche, S. D. (1994). *Between a Rock and a Hard Place: The At-Risk Student in the Open-Door College*. Washington, DC: Community College Press.

Roueche, J. E., & Roueche, S. D. (1999). *High Stakes, High Performance: Making Remedial Education Work*. Washington, DC: Community College Press.

Roueche, J. E. (1968). *Salvage, Redirection, or Custody? Remedial Education in the Community Junior College*. Washington, DC: American Association of Junior Colleges.

Roueche, J. E., Ely, E. E., & Roueche, S. D. (2001). *In Pursuit of Excellence: The Community College of Denver*. Washington, DC: Community College Press.

Rudner, L. (1994). Questions to Ask When Evaluating Tests. *Practical Assessment, Research & Evaluation*, 4 (2). Available: ERIC.

San Francisco State University. Tutoring at the LAC. Available: http://www.sfsu.edu/~lac/tuttraining.htm.

Saxon, D. P., & Boylan, H. R. (2001). Research and Issues Regarding the Cost of Remedial Education in Higher Education. Unpublished report prepared for the League for Innovation in the Community College.

Saxon, P., & Boylan, H. R. (1998). *Characteristics of Community College Remedial Students*. A literature review prepared for The League for Innovation in the Community College.

Saxon, P., & Boylan, H. R. (1998). *Outcomes of Remediation*. Paper prepared for The League for Innovation in the Community College.

Schults, C. (2000). *Remedial Education: Practices and Policies in Community Colleges*. Washington, DC: American Association of Community Colleges.

Scott, S. S., & Gregg, N. (2000, March/April). Meeting the Evolving Education Needs of Faculty Providing Access for College Students with LD. *Journal of Learning Disabilities*, 33 (2), 158-168. Available: EBSCO Academic Search Elite. 2881049. October 25, 2001.

Shaughnessy, M., & Moore, J. (1994). The KAIT with Developmental Students, Honor Students and Freshmen. *Psychology in the Schools*, 31, 286-287.

Shaughnessy, M. P. (1977). *Errors & Expectations. A Guide for the Teacher of Basic Writing*. New York: Oxford University Press.

Sheets, R. (1998). Names of Learning Centers. *Learning Support Centers in Higher Education*. Available: http://www.pvc.maricopa.edu/%7Elsche/about/names.htm

Shults, C. (2000). *Remedial Education: Practices and Policies in Community Colleges*. Research Brief. Washington DC: American Association of Community Colleges.

Simon, R. & Cannon, A. (2001, August 6). An Amazing Journey. *U. S. News & World Report*, pp. 11-18.

Smilkstein, R. (1999). Teaching Grammar the Way the Brain Learns Best. Available: http://www.umkc.edu/cad/nade/nadedocs/99conpap/rscpap99.htm.

Spann, M. G., Jr. (2000, February). *Remediation: A Must for the 21st Century Learning Society*. Policy Paper. Denver, CO: Education Commission of the States.

Spann, M. (2000, Fall). Rethinking Developmental Education: A Conversation with John N. Gardner. *Journal of Developmental Education*, 24 (1), 22-28.

Spann, N. (1990, Winter). Student Retention: An Interview with Vincent Tinto. *Journal of Developmental Education*, 14 (2), 18-24.

Stahl, N., Simpson, M., Hayes, C. (1992). Ten Recommendations from Research for Teaching High-Risk College Students. *Journal of Developmental Education*, 16 (1), 2-10.

Stansbury, S. (2001, Spring). Accelerated Learning Groups Enhance Supplemental Instruction for At-Risk Students. *Journal of Developmental Education*, 24 (3), 20-40.

Stewart, D., & Shamdasani, P. (1990). *Focus Groups: Theory and Practice*. Newbury Park, CA: Sage.

Stiplin, J. C. (2000). *A Review of Community College Curriculum Trends*. Los Angeles, CA: ERIC Clearinghouse for Community Colleges. Available: ERIC Document Reproduction Service No. ED 438 011.

Stratil, M. (1988). *College Student Inventory*. Iowa City, IA: USA Group Noel-Levitz.

Taylor, S. S. (2001, March). Bogged Down in the Basics? *Community College Week 13* (16), 6. Available: EBSCO Academic Search Elite. 4256959. August 1, 2001.

The Institute for Higher Education Policy. (1998). College Remediation. *The Journal of Higher Education*, 70 (2), 114-133.

The Texas Higher Education Coordinating Board. (2001). Texas Academic Skills Program. Available: http://www.tasp.nesinc.com.

Thompson, J. (1998, June). Developmental Students in Higher Education: Path Analysis of a National Sample. *College Student Journal*, 32, 499-510.

Tinto, V. (1998, January). Learning Communities and Developmental Education: Building Effective Educational Settings for All Students. Paper presented at the Conference on Replacing Remediation in Higher Education at Stanford University. Palo Alto, CA.

Tinto, V. (1997). Classrooms as Communities: Exploring the Educational Character of Student Persistence. *Journal of Higher Education*, 68 (6), 599-623.

Tinto, V. (1993). *Leaving College: Rethinking the Causes and Cures of Student Attrition*. 2nd ed. Chicago: The University of Chicago Press.

Upcraft, M., & Gardner, J. (1989). *The Freshman Year Experience*. San Francisco: Jossey-Bass.

Van, B. (1994). Learning Assistance Programs: Ingredients for Success. In M. Maxwell (Ed.), *Access to Success*. Clearwater, FL: H & H Publishing.

Vogt, P. (1993). *Dictionary of Statistics and Methodology*. Newbury Park, CA: Sage.

Wainer, H. (1990). *Computerized Adaptive Testing: A Primer.* Hillsdale, NJ: Lawrence Erlbaum.

Weiner, W. F., McVeigh, P., Clever, K., Brasington, D., & King, M.J. (1997). *Reinventing the Community College for the 21st Century Inquiry*. Virginia Community College System. Available: www.br.cc.va.us/vcca/i11wein.html.

Weinstein, C., Schulte, A., & Palmer, D. (1987). *Learning and Study Strategies Inventory*. Clearwater, FL: H & H Publishing.

Weissman, J., Bulakowski, C., & Jumisko, M. K. (1997, Winter). Using Research to Evaluate Developmental Education Programs and Policies. *New Directions for Community Colleges 100*, 73-80. Wilson Select Plus. Available: BEDI98001728. August 28, 2001.

Wrolstad, M. (2000, January 13). U. S. Population Projected to Double in Next Century. *Dallas Morning News*, p. 10A.

Zemelman, S., Daniels, H., & Hyde, A. (1998). *Best Practice New Standards for Teaching and Learning in America's Schools*. 2nd ed. Portsmouth, NH: Heinemann.

ABOUT THE AUTHOR

Robert McCabe is senior fellow with the League for Innovation in the Community College and former president of Miami-Dade Community College. In 40 years as a leader in higher education, he has been a consistent and forceful advocate for underprepared students. McCabe has written more than 100 articles, monographs, and book. His most ambitious project is the recently completed National Study of Community College Remedial Education, the basis for this report. McCabe has served on more than 70 educational boards, including the National Center for Public Policy and Higher Education, and he is a recipient of the American Association of Community College's Leadership Award.